The Layperson's Introduction to the Old Testament

ROBERT B. LAURIN

The Layperson's Introduction to the Old Testament

JUDSON PRESS® VALLEY FORGE

The Layperson's Introduction to the Old Testament

Library of Congress Cataloging-in-Publication Data
Laurin, Robert B. (Robert Bruce), 1927-1977.
[Layman's introduction to the Old Testament]
The layperson's introduction to the Old Testament / Robert B. Laurin.
p. cm.
Previously published under title: The layman's introduction to the Old Testament.
Includes bibliographical references.
ISBN 0-8170-1163-3
1. Bible. O.T. —Introductions. I. Title
BS1140.2.L37 1991
221.6—dc20 90-22713

Printed in the U.S.A.
96 97 98 99 00 01 02 03 9 8 7 6 5 4 3 2

PREFACE TO THE REVISED EDITION

When we decided to let *The Layman's Introduction to the Old Testament* go out of print, we thought that it was nearing the end of its productive life and would soon be supplanted by newer books. But as requests for the book kept coming, it became apparent that we had underestimated the staying power of Dr. Laurin's "little volume." With its concise overview of the Old Testament, its basic explanation and incorporation of biblical criticism, and its illumination of major Old Testament themes, the book met a need. And so, we decided to bring it back to life as *The Layperson's Introduction to the Old Testament.*

Dr. Laurin's text has been revised and updated to reflect some of the changes our language has undergone in the past two decades. The bibliographic references that follow each chapter have been amended and now include some of the many fine books on the Old Testament that have been published in the intervening years. The essential content of the book, however, remains the same, as relevant today as it was when it was first published.

It is our hope that *The Layperson's Introduction to the Old Testament* will continue to be a valuable resource for many years to come.

The Editors

PREFACE

This little volume is intended to provide for the person who is not a specialist in biblical matters a guide to understanding the structure and significance of the Old Testament. This portion of the Scriptures was the Bible of the early Christians, the source from which they drew much of their instruction, and the background against which they viewed the life and work of Jesus. In addition to this fact, the Old Testament is also part of our Bible today, and it contains a wealth of material which bears upon our personal, social, and political life.

Partly because the idiom of the Old Testament is difficult, its meaning is not always clear, and its structure at times is confusing, the Old Testament has often been neglected by Christians. Consequently, this book seeks to offer directions by which people may comprehend what they read as they pursue their own studies through the text. One cannot read the Old Testament straight through as a continuous narrative. It is divided into various kinds of literature, not arranged in strict chronological order, nor with the same specific purpose. This handbook seeks to keep the reader oriented to history, style, chronological structure, and purpose of the various Old Testament books. Therefore, the question of explicit contemporary meaning has not provided the major focus, since this must usually be determined by a particular individual or group in a given situation. The book is meant, rather, to give a summary of the results of scholarly study that have illuminated the significance of the text. Thus with this book and the Bible at hand, the reader may come to encounter more profoundly the God who seeks to speak through the pages of the Bible a word that affects one's life in the present age and in one's own situation.

CONTENTS

INTRODUCTION

In all the affairs of life where communication is intended, one asks, often unconsciously, "What kind of information am I expected to gain from the document I am reading or the words I am hearing?" For example, a person who receives in the mail an advertisement for travel to Hawaii does not expect information about the topography of Scotland or about the ecumenical movement, but only about what the travel brochure intends. The determination of intent or purpose must also apply to the Old Testament if one is to avoid seeking answers to questions with which the text does not deal.

WHAT IS THE OLD TESTAMENT?

On the surface, the Old Testament is a collection of writings gathered by the Israelite people that contains traditions about their history covering a period of almost two thousand years. But, more basically, the Old Testament is a collection of writings designed to show God's involvement in the world and to bring men and women to respond to and encounter this God in their daily life. Let us see what this means.

1. First of all, the Old Testament is a *history.* It describes the major events or periods in the life of an ancient people called the Israelites. It tells the story of their origin, development, and response to life. Now it is to be noted that it is not a history of a "race" but of a "people." The difference is important, and yet many moderns have not understood this. A "race" is a group of

individuals with similar physical and perhaps psychological characteristics. From the start the Israelites were a "mixed multitude" (Exodus 12:38) containing a mixture of many racial groups (Genesis 41:50; Numbers 12:1; Nehemiah 13:23-24; Ezekiel 16:3). Thus any attempt to identify an Israelite by physical characteristics is impossible. The Israelites were a "people," that is, a group of individuals who shared a common Middle Eastern habitat, language, way of life, and religious tradition. In a similar way one can speak of the "American people," but not of the "American race." The Old Testament, then, is the story of an aggregate of ancient persons who were bound together by a common cultural experience, particularly, as we shall see, by their relationship with God.

The story of this people is that of a group who appeared relatively late on the scene of events in the Middle East. The evidence of civilization there goes back to around 7000 B.C., but Abraham, the father of the Israelites, did not arrive until perhaps 1900 B.C. Great city-states had fought for thousands of years over the territory into which Abraham wandered. The city from which Abraham came, Ur, was already an ancient site in his day. In Egypt the pyramids had already experienced centuries of weathering by sand and wind. Mesopotamia and Egypt had witnessed remarkably advanced cultural achievements, but Abraham was only a seminomadic merchant, and his descendants were never, except for a brief period, much more than this. Why is a history about nomads and shepherds so significant? We shall see why in just a moment.

Outwardly Israel's history is not very distinguished. After migrating from Mesopotamia, Abraham established his family in Canaan around 1900 B.C. For a few centuries life revolved around the selling and trading of livestock. But at some time during the days of a man named Jacob, the Israelites, due to severe famine, fled to Egypt. There the annual overflow of the Nile provided for a more dependable crop. Although at first the Israelites were received hospitably, later they were thrown into slavery and forced to work for the Egyptians. But early in the thirteenth century B.C. they escaped into the Sinai desert under the leadership of Moses. Through long years of wandering in the desert, and particularly after an encounter with God at Mount Sinai, the Israelite slaves became hardened into a disciplined community. Thus they were able to move from the desert into the land of Canaan under the military leadership of Joshua and to achieve at least a partial occupation of the land. For some time they existed in tribal units scattered around the country. Loosely unified by their common loyalty to the Lord, they were able to join forces in time of military threat. But there was no central political authority, and thus no real stability. So it was that in the last part of the eleventh century B.C., because of military subjugation by the Philistines, the people asked the prophet Samuel to anoint a king to provide them with the centralization they had lacked and to throw off the power of the Philistines.

Saul became the first king, but his whole reign was spent at war with the Philistines and other groups. Living like some ancient Robin Hood, he was never able to achieve decisive victory. His successor, David (1000–961 B.C.), conquered the Philistines and established a single kingdom over the whole of western Palestine. By making Jerusalem the political capital and the religious center, he welded the loyalties of the scattered tribes together. But only during his reign, and during the rule of his son Solomon, did the Israelites achieve political importance. This period was Israel's "golden age." However, Solomon (961–922 B.C.), although skilled in diplomacy and commerce, was not wise in internal policies. His heavy taxation measures, his grandiose building projects, and his policy of forced labor weakened the loyalties of the mass of people. So at his death, ten of the northern tribes revolted under the leadership of Jeroboam and established the kingdom of Israel with its capital being eventually at Samaria. The two remaining tribes (Benjamin and Judah) became the kingdom of Judah centered at Jerusalem. The subsequent history of these two monarchies, apart from a few exceptions, became one of growing religious apostasy and social oppression, coupled with futile attempts to play the game of power politics with surrounding countries.

Almost inevitably, in 721 B.C., Israel was swallowed up by the Assyrian empire, with her population largely displaced by peoples from other Assyrian vassal states. Judah paid tribute to the Assyrians and was able to last a little longer in a semi-independent condition. But Judah finally fell, in 587 B.C., before the Babylonian armies. The capital city, Jerusalem, and the temple were destroyed, and the elite and artisans were driven to exile in Babylonia. The overthrow of the Babylonians by Cyrus the Persian in 539 B.C. enabled many of the exiles to return to Palestine and to attempt to rebuild their shattered homes, fields, and cities. Much progress was made. Jerusalem's walls were restored, and the temple was rebuilt. But Israel was still a vassal to the Persians, governed by the high priest. Israel's political glory was past. Persian rule was followed by Greek control in 331 B.C., and for this period the biblical record is virtually silent. We know from materials mostly outside the Bible that when the Greeks attempted to enforce pagan religious practices on the Jews in 167 B.C., a revolt was fomented. After a series of skirmishes the Jews won a measure of independence (142–63 B.C.). But this too was lost because of corruption and the military might of Rome. The Jews never again were independent until the twentieth century.

A major cause of Israel's political troubles lay in its geographical position. Situated on the Levant Coast of the Mediterranean, Palestine forms a part of what is usually called the "Fertile Crescent." This is a great sickle-shaped area of cultivable land that stretches northward from the head of the Persian Gulf through the Mesopotamian Valley to the foot of the mountains that form the southern border of modern-day Turkey. It then moves across to the Mediterranean and from there down through Syria and Palestine to the border of Egypt. At either end of this "crescent" are rich agricultural areas (the Nile valley and Mesopotamia), and in these lands powerful civilizations developed. It was the fate of Palestine and the Levant Coast to form the only usable bridge between these areas. All commerce from Egypt to Mesopotamia, or vice versa, and from Egypt to Asia Minor had to pass through Palestine. The Arabian desert was impassable, and shipping on the Mediterranean had not been developed. Consequently, the history of the area was one of continual struggle on the part of the major powers at either end of the Fertile Crescent to control the trade bridge of Palestine. The Israelites, therefore, were constantly facing the threat of invading forces, and their size and economic resources were never sufficient, except for the brief period under David and Solomon, to resist the invaders.

2. A second major thing to understand about the collection of traditions called the Old Testament is that it is *a theology of history.* It is not simply a chronicle of events; no true history is this. Every historian sets out to interpret, either consciously or unconsciously by the materials selected, the significance of the events recorded. This is true of the biblical writers. They had a "theological" interpretation. They sought to show that the events of life, particularly those in which Israel participated, disclosed the purposes of God and involved the presence of God. They wrote in order to lead their readers to encounter this God and to discover God's character and will.

The theological perspective comes out in the way an event is described or in comments made about that event. This can be seen in the description of the escape from Egypt under the leadership of Moses. In terms of world history it was an extremely minor incident—a few thousand slaves fled from their masters. It is not even mentioned in Egyptian records, although one would not really expect it to be. The Egyptian pharaohs did not leave behind histories of their reigns, that is, accounts showing how various events shaped the course of their rule. Egyptian monuments list only victorious military campaigns; defeats are omitted. The loss of a few slaves would have passed unrecorded. Although it was an incidental irritation in the eyes of the Egyptians, it was the most significant event in their whole history to the Israelites. To the Israelite historians, Israel's escape from Egypt was not just an escape; it was a deliverance by God. So at the beginning of the Ten Commandments we read: "I am the LORD your God, who brought you out of the land of Egypt, out of the house of bondage" (Exodus 20:2). And why did God bring them out? "You have seen what I did to the Egyptians, and how I bore you on eagles' wings and brought you to myself. Now therefore, if you will obey my voice and keep my covenant, you shall be my own possession among all peoples; for all the earth is mine, and you shall be to me a kingdom of priests and a holy nation" (Exodus 19:4-6). God had called Israel to be a priestly mediator to the rest of the world (see also Genesis 12:1-4; 2 Samuel 17:14; Isaiah 44:28).

It is extremely important to remember as one reads the Old Testament that it is a history written from the perspective of faith in God. The materials have been selected and described in order to present a theology of history. The Old Testament writers were not usually concerned with the questions the natural scientist would ask, nor with ones the philosopher would pose. They were seeking to answer the theological questions about the meaning and destiny of human existence in a world ruled by God. Therefore, they did not speculate about the details of the origin and structure of the world, nor about the existence or essence of God. They assumed God is, and they were interested in showing how and why God is at work in our world.

3. A third thing to understand about the Old Testament is that it is *an artistic history.* A reader should not facilely assume that the whole Old Testament is history in the technical sense of the word. It contains an abundance of different kinds of literature, much of it "historical," but not all of it. There are large sections of songs, sermons, maxims, and other types of material. In other words, the collection called the Old Testament includes a selection of the different kinds of literature used by the Israelites throughout their history. It is important to grasp the fact that these pieces of literature, coming from the different periods of Israel's history, all share in the common purpose of interpreting the meaning of life under God. The songs extol the work of God in history (for example, Psalm 78); the sermons exhort persons to be obedient to God (for example, Amos 5:14-15); the maxims seek to relate all of humanity's everyday affairs to God (for example, Proverbs 1:7); and, as we saw, so do the historical narratives.

So, then, what is the Old Testament? It is a collection of writings designed to show God's involvement in the world and to get persons to respond to this God. The purpose of the Old Testament is not simply to impart information. It is rather that by this information about God's character and will, people might be brought to an encounter with God in daily life. The apostle John said of his Gospel: "These are written that you may believe that Jesus is the Christ, the Son of God, and that believing you may have life in his name" (John 20:31). Something similar could be said of the Old Testament. It is both a record and a medium—a *record* of God's involvement in the world and a *medium* through which God seeks to meet us and have us respond and find life.

HOW DOES ONE READ THE OLD TESTAMENT?

It is crucial to remember that in reading the Old Testament one is not dealing with some magical document unrelated to other pieces of literature. Just as God's revelation took on human form in Christ, it has also been clothed in human speech and writing. Because of this, therefore, one has to investigate the Old Testament by the literary methods appropriate for any other piece of literature. One has to determine how it was put together, the time and culture from which the various parts came, the meaning of ancient idioms and words, and the forms in which these are expressed.

1. The Composite Character. The Old Testament is not a unified book, but an anthology or great collection of separate books. Most of the individual books within the collection are the products of more than one person. This knowledge immediately tells us something about reading the Old Testament. We do not attempt to read it as we would a novel or biography, that is, from beginning to end as if we were reading a developing plot or chronological account. We read it selectively, trying to find groups of material which have a common relationship or looking for discussions of special topics or particular events.

The versions of the Old Testament in general use today are structured around three clusters of materials. The first cluster contains *the historical and legal texts,* Genesis through Esther, a total of seventeen books. Actually, as we shall see, Genesis 1–11 is a preface sketching prehistoric times, and Genesis 12 begins a series of accounts tracing events in the life of Israel from about 1900 B.C. to 350 B.C. The reader must always keep in mind that this section of the Old Testament is not an historical account in the modern sense of the word. We saw that the Old Testament writers present a "theology of history." Thus, there will be a high degree of selectivity in the materials presented, and the events that they record will be seen through eyes of faith in God. They were not interested in giving us an account of everything that happened, but in showing us how certain events illustrate the work of God in history. Furthermore, the historical account does not move forward with unbroken narration. It is interrupted by songs (for example, Exodus 15:1-18; 2 Samuel 1:19-27), poems (1 Samuel 15:22-23; Joshua 10:12-13), laws (Exodus 20:22–23:33; Leviticus 1–7), and so on. Sometimes stories are repeated in slightly different form (for example, Genesis 12:10–13:1 and 20:1-18). And there are even duplicate accounts of a whole period in Israel's life. The events described in First and Second Samuel and First and Second Kings are described again in First and Second Chronicles from a different point of view.

We are familiar with this approach from our reading of the Gospels in the New Testament. They, too, present a "theology of history"; in particular, they give us the theological meaning of the events in Christ's life. And in the Gospels we find the narrative interrupted by various kinds of literature (for example, the Sermon on the Mount in Matthew 5–7) as well as the repetition of stories and events from different points of view.

The second cluster of material contains *the song and wisdom texts.* These are the five books from Job through the Song of Songs. In general they contain a collection of personal and corporate responses to the events described in the first section. Here one finds prayers and songs of many types and moods, advice about the conduct of everyday affairs, discussions about the significance of life—all in reaction to particular problems in Israel's history. We are not always able to identify the specific problems reflected in this literature, but we can usually discover the kind of problems.

So here we find quite a different type of literature than we found in the first cluster, and to be aware of this difference is to be prepared to read with great understanding. Not only are the themes usually different, but also most of the material is in poetic form. When one moves from Esther to Job, it is almost as if one had changed from one part of a library to another, from the works of history to the books on poetry and philosophy. There is nothing in the New Testament quite like this section. The prayers, songs, wise sayings, and discussions about the meaning of life are only scattered here and there throughout the body of New Testament books.

The third cluster contains *the prophetic and apocalyptic texts.* These are Isaiah through Malachi, a total of seventeen books. This material deals not only with the social, religious, and political problems of Israel's history from the eighth century B.C. onward, but also with the goal of the historical process. In a general sense the prophets provide us with a commentary on their contemporary events in light of the will of God, in particular as that will has been explicated in the Law. Often they were messengers of doom. They arose in times of crisis when the future of the nation of Israel was held in balance and saw only darkness in the immediate days. They were not without hope, but that was beyond the moment of their times.

There is one book in this third section which is different from the rest—the Book of Daniel. It is an "apocalypse," that is, a "revelation" or "disclosure" of last things. Its mood is different from the prophetic books. The prophets saw the evils of Israelite society and sought to denounce the people and urge them to repent. But the Book of Daniel saw the world at large as evil and as persecuting the innocent Israelites. Its purpose was to encourage all Israelites to resist and to remain faithful to the Lord.

The prophetic and apocalyptic materials have their New Testament counterpart. The book of Acts and the Epistles record the message and life of those who had been sent by Jesus Christ to preach the gospel to the world. In similar fashion the prophets were "messengers" of the Lord, sent to proclaim divine will in their society. The book of Revelation is similar to the Book of Daniel.

2. The Problem of the Canon. The church has not always agreed about this structure of the Old Testament, nor about its contents. The Roman Catholics, for example, include seven more books in the collection than the Protestants or the Jews, plus some additional material in Esther and Daniel. This extra literature is called the "apocryphal" (hidden or spurious) writings by the Protestants, but the "deuterocanonical" (second canonical) writings by the Roman Catholics. One can see that there is quite a difference of opinion as to the authority of this extra material. How are we to understand this? Why do Protestants and Roman Catholics differ? Were there other materials that did not get in either Old Testament collection? How did our Old Testament materials come to be selected and arranged the way they are?

That the present Old Testament is the result of a long process of selectivity is evident from its own pages. The biblical writers refer to other pieces of literature which were extant in their own day. Sometimes they quote from them (Joshua 10:13; 2 Samuel 1:18), and sometimes they refer the reader to these sources for more information (2 Kings 14:28; 15:11). But, for some reason, the Israelites did not include these sources in their sacred Scriptures or "canon," that is, in their authoritative collection of writings that give witness to God and divine will. Why? We do not know exactly, but we can recognize that through the years there came a gradual acceptance by the majority of Israelites that certain of their traditions proclaimed the Word of God while others did not. Apparently it was largely something that was "felt," rather than "specified." The matter came to a head at the end of the first century A.D. At this time some leading Jewish rabbis gathered at the small Palestinian town of Jamnia to discuss, among other matters, the extent of the authoritative writings. The pressure of Christianity's claims of further revelation from God had begun to be felt. Some small Jewish sects were also circulating new writings that told about the future. So in order to set their scriptural house in order, these rabbis sought to come to some common mind on what Judaism as a whole accepted as authoritative. Here the three basic sections of the Jewish Bible—the Law, Prophets, and Writings—were affirmed as generally accepted.

Jesus and the early church accepted the Old Testament as the Word of God (John 10:35), and for a few centuries it was the only Bible of the church. But there has never been agreement in the church as to the limits of the Old Testament. The difficulty arises over the fact that the New Testament never defines the contents of the second and third sections of the Jewish canon. Jesus spoke of things written about him in "the Law of Moses," in "the prophets," and in "the Psalms." But he did not delineate the contents of any of these. There has never been any dispute about the "Law," but even Judaism indicates uncertainty about the other two. On the one hand, there were various small groups of Jews scattered around Palestine using different collections. The Dead Sea Scrolls have shown us this very clearly. Many nonbiblical books were found among the scrolls, but there is no real indication that they were considered of less authority than our biblical writings. On the other hand, in the world outside Palestine various Jews were also using more than our present books. For example, the Septuagint, a Greek version produced among Greek-speaking Jews in Egypt between 250 and 100 B.C., contains more material than that found in the Old Testament accepted by the Jews at Jamnia. In fact there is no single Septuagint "canon," since the various manuscripts differ in the books they include. The church for many centuries struggled over this, and it was not really until 1546, during the Reformation, that an official stand was taken. The Protestants in the main accepted the Palestinian collection, while the Roman Catholic church continued to use a canon of seven more books, plus additions to Daniel and Esther. The Greek Orthodox church has also had its own tradition and accepts a collection which is a bit different than either of the other two. Present-day Judaism accepts the same books as the Protestants, but arranges them differently.

There will probably never be agreement about the canon, and perhaps this is good. It tends to remind us that when all is said and done the Old Testament is authoritative to us not because some official body decreed it to be, but because, as with the people of God through the years, we come to encounter the living God through it. Humanity can never box God in and claim that God can only speak in one way. So there have been various traditions about the text. When we read the Old Testament, therefore, we read a collection that has grown slowly through the years and reflects this process of growth in not being structured neatly. But we read the record of a God who intends to encounter us and speak to us in the present time.

3. The Literary Character. Just as the Old Testament is not uniform in structure, neither is it consistent in form and style of writing. There is not only a mixture of prose and poetry, but also a wide variety of kinds of prose and poetry. This knowledge also tells us something important about reading the Old Testament. We do not read all the Old Testament literature in the same way or on the same level of expression. Each part must be defined if its contents are to be understood as the author intended. There is an analogy here to the newspaper. The front-page news is reported in a different way than that on the editorial page; the latter contains much more interpretation than the former. And when reading the comic section, one knows from the start that it is fantasy, so that when a character dies, one does not mourn the loss of a real individual.

Understanding the literary style of the Old Testament is helped by realizing that it comes from an ancient Near Eastern culture, and also that much of it originated in spoken situations. This means that we must be cautious about investing twentieth-century notions into the words of the authors. We must look on the world as they saw it—without the advantage of the scientific advances that we know. We must read their words from the perspective of their culture, not only in terms of the images or symbols they used that reflect nomadic and agricultural ways of life, but also in regard to their penchant for figurative expression. Metaphor, hyperbole, and symbol abound in the language of that time.

Let us consider an illustration. One of the central events of the Old Testament is the Israelites' deliverance from Egyptian slavery under Moses. Throughout the text, authors made many allusions to this event and described it in a variety of ways, as shown by the following examples:

a. *Theological description* (Exodus 14:21-25, 28). "Then Moses stretched out his hand over the sea; and the LORD drove the sea back by a strong east wind all night, and made the sea dry land, and the waters were divided. And the people of Israel went into the midst of the sea on dry ground, the waters being a wall to them on their right hand and on their left. The Egyptians pursued, and went in after them into the midst of the sea, all Pharaoh's horses, his chariots, and his horsemen. And in the morning watch the LORD in the pillar of fire and of cloud looked down upon the host of the Egyptians, and discomfited the host of the Egyptians, clogging their chariot wheels so that they drove heavily; and the Egyptians said, 'Let us flee from before Israel; for the LORD fights for them against the Egyptians.' . . . The waters returned and covered the chariots and the horsemen and all the host of Pharaoh that had followed them into the sea; not so much as one of them remained."

b. *Hymnic glorification* (Exodus 15:1-2, 4-5, 8, 12).

basic will and kind of life. The Bible is like a novel in this regard. The plot is laid in the Old Testament, and much of the action takes place there. But the denouement comes in the New Testament; at least a part of the unfolding of the story comes there. The final resolution is still awaited. So we cannot read the Bible and neglect the Old Testament any more than we can read a major novel or biography and skip the first two-thirds of the book. All parts contribute to the understanding of the whole. This can be seen by structuring the whole Bible as one great story in three parts, each of which has historical as well as contemporary significance.

1. Genesis 1–11. The biblical story begins with a prologue of eleven chapters in which the basic problem of life is established: Humankind has been formed by a sovereign God to find fulfillment through participating in a divine-human partnership of creative activity, but is in revolt against God and is reaping disorder and disunity. The rest of the Bible is concerned with showing how this problem is being resolved by God. As we shall see later, Genesis 1–11 was written after Israel had come into existence as a people and was intended to answer the question: "Why was Israel called by God as a special people?" Genesis 1–11 answers by saying: "Because humankind needs help to become what it was intended to become." So Genesis 1–11 is a theological treatise disclosing for us the purpose and need of humanity. It does this in two ways. It describes, first of all, what *was* at the beginning of time. But, second, it describes what *is* true of all people ever since, true of our day. In other words, all the events in this prologue are typical examples of what all people are like. The events are meant to be object lessons for all of us in every age to read and learn about ourselves. Thus, each year Israel repeated the ancient story of creation and preserved its primeval stories; they were repeated as if "today" they were happening again (see Deuteronomy 5:3; Psalm 103). God not only created humanity a long time ago in God's own image; but also has created everyone in that divine image (see Psalm 8). You and I were born to fulfill God's purposes in this world, to do God's will, to complete God's creation. Since this purpose would not be meaningful unless we can choose it ourselves, God has not forced it upon us but has given us the choice. And we have done what those original people did: We have chosen to rebel and we have sinned and thwarted God's purposes.

2. Genesis 12–Malachi. The key to this second part of the Bible is found in Genesis 12:1-3. God called Abram (Abraham) and his descendants as servants to bring "blessing" to the whole world, that is, to bring to humankind what it was created to have—wholeness and fulfillment. Thus Genesis 12 to Malachi is simply the story of God's further creative work in the world, still with humanity's (Israel's) help, to bring the goal of creation to completion. It is the story of God's solution to human rebellion and disorder, and again it is a theological treatise with a twofold purpose. It describes on the one hand, what *was,* what happened to a people called Israel. And, on the other hand, it showed how these events disclosed the purposes of God for all people.

The Old Testament contains a series of selected pieces of literature that illustrate God's persistent efforts to bring humankind to creation's goal. This means that the whole Old Testament is always moving toward a goal; yet it is a goal that is only seen and promised and partially fulfilled but is never attained. We learn of God at work in history, but not of God completing that work. This means that the form of Israel's life was always intended to be temporary until the relationship with God would embrace all humanity. God began at creation with a purpose for all people; Israel was one means for achieving that goal (see Isaiah 42:6-7; 45:22-23). So the story of the Old Testament is the story of a missionary people. At least they were intended to be so, and their possession of land and king and temple was only meant to be reflective of a greater form of life that would involve all humankind. But Israel refused to be that missionary body. It settled down into a typical materialistic, nationalistic existence—religious on the surface, but not at the core. It sought to be great in ways that were not open to it geographically or economically. It sought to be a great political power when it was intended to be a great spiritual power. This is the burden of some of the prophetic books—Israel had turned its back on the very reason for its formation as a people. As the Book of Jonah illustrates, Israel's great sin was not simply immorality or idolatry, but insularity; it was the refusal to reach outside its borders with the knowledge of God. And so Israel lost both national existence and power. We shall see that a few of the prophets (for example, Zechariah) did not always understand this universalistic concern.

The record of Genesis 12 through Malachi, on the other hand, deals with what *is* important today. The real reason this section of the Old Testament is used in the church is not because of historical interest in a people called Israel, but because God's worldwide purposes were revealed through them. Israel's message and relationship with God were always intended to be for all people. If the Old Testament is part of the same story we read in the New, then its witness to the various facets of the divine-human relationship are as relevant today as they ever were. This is why the early church could continue to use the Old Testament as its Bible—the same God who was revealed in Jesus Christ had disclosed the divine will and way during the Old Testament period. Indeed, the author of Hebrews says just this: "In many and various ways God spoke of old to our fathers by the prophets; but in these last days he has spoken to us by a Son . . ." (Hebrews 1:1-2).

Now there is obviously much in the Old Testament that is different and no longer relevant. Its form of political, social, and cultic life has gone. No longer are the structures of Old Testament sacrifice, feast, and tithe part of the Christian way of life. No longer are many of its legal requirements meaningful to the church (notice Exodus 21:15, 17; Deuteronomy 21:18-21). The coming of Christ has brought a new covenant or "arrangement." Paul writes: "Why then the law? It was added because of transgressions, till the offspring should come to whom the promise had been made," that is, until Christ should come (Galatians 3:19). However, though the form of life has changed, and though some of the cultural ideas of Old Testament writers have gone, the intent and goal of life expressed remains. Is this not the present church's approach to the New Testament as well? The first-century way of life has been abandoned, along with some of its culturally influenced ideas, but its proclamation about the work of God and the needed response of people remains.

3. Matthew–Revelation. With the New Testament record we learn of further, decisive steps by God to complete God's worldwide concerns. But the New Testament, as well as the Old, has a twofold purpose for the church. It depicts initially what *was* in the first century. It speaks of the birth, life, death, and resurrection of Jesus Christ and relates the formation of the church. But the New Testament is more than a historical document; it is also a theological treatise. So the coming of Christ is seen as another major creative act of God. Through Jesus Christ, the "Word" through whom all things were made (John 1:1-18), the church is "created" (Ephesians 2:10), and the individual believer is made a "new creation" (2 Corinthians 5:17). It is through Christ that the goal of creation is completed. This is why Paul can write that "all the promises of God find their Yes in him" (2 Corinthians 1:20).

The purpose that God began in creation and carried forward through the long and frustrating years of Israel's history has come to completion in Jesus Christ. He is the end of the story, its denouement; he is the seed of Abraham through whom all the world will be blessed. On this basis Christ and the apostles used the Old Testament as part of their message. They saw themselves in a line with the Old Testament, as the fulfillment of its promises, as part of the same people of God (Acts 15:14-18; Romans 4:13-15; 9:6-8, 24-26; Galatians 3:28-29; 1 Peter 2:9). God's revelation in Christ was not to do away with God's revelation to Israel, but to fulfill and complete it. Thus, while the Bible contains both the Old and the New Testaments, it is one story.

- What was it about Israel's geographical and economic situation that prohibited it from being great politically? Wherein, then, did its potential greatness lie? How does this help us to determine how our own country is to strive for its role in the world?
- Why is it important for us to have a canon? Should other books be added? Why?
- What is the primary purpose of the Old Testament? In light of this purpose, what are some ways in which we may expect it to speak to the contemporary situation?

Additional Resources

Anderson, Bernhard W. *Understanding the Old Testament.* 4th ed. Englewood Cliffs, N.J.: Prentice Hall, 1986.

Beckwith, Roger. *The Old Testament Canon of the New Testament Church.* Grand Rapids: William B. Eerdmans, 1986.

Boadt, Lawrence. *Reading the Old Testament: An Introduction.* New York: Paulist Press, 1984.

Bright, John. *A History of Israel.* 3rd ed. Philadelphia: Westminster Press, 1981.

Bruce, Frederick F. *The Books and the Parchments.* Rev. ed. Westwood, N.J.: Fleming H. Revell Co., 1963.

Brueggemann, Walter, and Wolff, H. W. *The Vitality of Old Testament Traditions.* 2nd ed. Atlanta: John Knox Press, 1982.

Campbell, Antony F. *Study Companion to Old Testament Literature: An Approach to Writings of Pre-Exilic Israel.* Wilmington, Del.: Michael Glazier, 1989.

Childs, Brevard S. *Introduction to the Old Testament as Scripture.* Philadelphia: Fortress Press, 1979.

de Vaux, Roland. *Ancient Israel: Its Life and Institutions.* Vol. 1, *Social Institutions.* Vol. 2, *Religious Institutions.* New York: McGraw-Hill, 1965.

Hayes, John H., and Miller, J. Maxwell, eds. *Israelite and Judean History.* Philadelphia: Westminster Press, 1977.

Heaton, E. W. *Everyday Life in Old Testament Times.* New York: Charles Scribner's Sons, 1956.

May, Herbert G., ed. *Oxford Bible Atlas.* 3rd ed. New York: Oxford University Press, 1985.

Rowley, Harold H. *The Unity of the Bible.* Philadelphia: Westminster Press, 1955.

Schmidt, Werner H. *The Faith of the Old Testament: A History.* Translated by John Sturdy. Philadelphia: Westminster Press, 1983.

Soggin, J. Alberto. *Introduction to the Old Testament.* 3rd ed. Translated by John Bowden. Louisville: Westminster/John Knox Press, 1989.

Wurthwein, Ernst. *The Text of the Old Testament.* Translated by Erroll F. Rhodes. Grand Rapids: William B. Eerdmans, 1979.

1

THE PRIESTLY HISTORY

Genesis–Numbers

The first major cluster of materials in the Old Testament—the historic and legal texts—went through a long process of growth and arrangement from various sources. Many of these sources had lived for centuries in oral form. Songs were sung at harvest, at worship, or following a military victory. Laws were formed to settle some boundary dispute or to establish some liturgical procedure. Maxims were recited in some business or family situation. Stories were told, often with musical accompaniment, to explain customs or place names, or to extol the military feats of some hero. This original oral situation is reflected in the Old Testament, for example, in one of the oldest pieces of literature in the Old Testament—a victory song (circa 1200 B.C.) eulogizing the military exploits of Deborah (Judges 5). The oral transmission is also reflected in an introduction formula, "Hear, O Israel, the statutes and ordinances which I speak in your hearing this day . . ." (Deuteronomy 5:1).

Writing was also known and used from Israel's earliest days. Gideon assumed that children knew how to read and write (Judges 8:14). There have been many ancient archives and libraries uncovered by archaeologists in the various countries of the Middle East. Laws, records, and liturgical forms were most naturally committed to writing on stone, leather, or papyrus. Jeremiah dictated a selection of his oracles to his secretary Baruch (Jeremiah 36).

Both oral and written materials provided the sources for our present historical and legal texts. Somewhere along the line a few events or laws (particularly those that dealt with a common theme or person) would be gathered together and remembered or recorded. The clusters of stories about Abraham, Jacob, Moses, or David and the collection of various laws must have come this way. Several reasons explain this process of grouping. Sometimes stories about famous figures in Israel's past were collected. With great joy, for example, Israelites told how the nomad Abram got the best of the sophisticated Egyptians and how his wife was far prettier than the Egyptian women (Genesis 12:10-20). At other times, the traditions were collected to be used for recitation in public worship. Exodus 15:1-18 is an indication that historical traditions were used in such a way. Still another reason for collecting materials was to provide proof that Israel had legal right to its settled territories. The authors sought to show that they were the recipients of land promised by God. For example, a comment on the conquest of Palestine by the Israelites is recorded in Joshua 21:45: "Not one of all the good promises which the LORD had made to the house of Israel had failed; all came to pass." The story of David's rise (1 Samuel 16:4–2 Samuel 5:25) probably was collected for a similar reason—to offer justification for the transfer of kingship from Saul to David.

The final editing of the traditions or collections of traditions that make up our present historical and legal texts took place largely because of theological reasons. The authors were attempting to show the religious lessons to be gained from the major historical periods of Israel's existence. We shall see more of this later.

On occasion the source material used by the writers and editors of the present books is named. Numbers 21:14-15, for example, is a quote from "The Book of the Wars of the LORD." The editor of First Kings reminds the readers that for further information about the topic at hand they can refer to "The Book of the Chronicles of the Kings of Israel" (1 Kings 14:19).

Most of the time, however, the different sources are not named. In spite of this, scholars are often able to identify such sources by various stylistic peculiarities and to suggest the period in Israel's history from which they came. Three famous sources were used in the formation of the bulk of Genesis through Numbers. The first is called the "J" source because it tends to use consistently the proper name "Jahweh" (usually spelled "Yahweh") for God; it probably comes from the tenth century B.C. during the reign of Solomon. The second source is called the "E" source because it uses the name "Elohim" for God, and perhaps comes from the Northern Kingdom of Israel about a century later, that is, in the ninth century B.C. shortly after the breakup of Solomon's kingdom. The third source is termed the "P" source because of its dominant priestly interest in worship and law; it appears to have been gathered together during the exile in Babylonia in the sixth century B.C. Other smaller sources in Genesis through Numbers have been discovered, but a great deal of dispute has arisen about their scope. One other important source comprises the major part of the book of Deuteronomy (except for the last four chapters) and is appropriately named "D." It arose as a collection sometime in the first part of the seventh century B.C.

Scholars who divide the historical and legal material into various sources use a series of criteria. They do not simply look for the use of a particular name for God, but for a series of expressions or designations for persons, places, and objects that consistently appear together. When we read novels or other pieces of literature, we also recognize this. We are aware of the fact that there are stylistic differences between Winston Churchill and Arnold Toynbee. Their choices of particular words, their repetitions of expressions, their phrasings, and their presuppositions help us to distinguish between their writings. It is, of course, often impossible to tell whether Churchill or Toynbee wrote a given paragraph or sentence, but with a more extended amount of material, particularly if the same subject is dealt with twice, such a distinction becomes easier. The point is that although stylistic variations are often difficult to spot, it is clear that different writers have different styles. The same is true with the biblical sources.

The discovery that the composition of the historical and legal books was a long process involving many sources means various things for the readers of the Old Testament. *First,* this recognition of sources helps us to understand why certain narratives and laws appear more than once and why they do not always agree with one another. Often these repeated accounts come from different sources. Because each contributed something the other did not, the editors wisely placed both in the text and did not attempt to harmonize them. The narrative of Abraham's journey to Egypt, for example, occurs twice, and there are various differences between the two (Genesis 12:10-20; 20:1-18). The first account comes from the "J" source, while the second is from "E." Now it is not impossible that such a thing happened twice so similarly. What is more plausible, however, is that there was one event, but it was preserved in two traditions. Since the editors were not interested in making all the details agree, they kept both accounts. Each stressed in its own way the important point of the keeping of God's promise to Abraham. We are familiar with this phenomenon from the New Testament. In the Gospels we often find three or four accounts of the same event in the life of Christ, and each differs in details from the others. In the New Testament the duplicate accounts appear side by side in separate books. In the Old Testament they have been brought together into one book.

Second, the recognition of sources shows us that the main characters of the books are the heroes, not the authors. Even though a given book may bear the name of Moses or Samuel or Joshua, this does not mean that it is the product of his hand. The books are all anonymous, the products of centuries of gradual collection. For example, the first five books of the Old Testament, called the "Pentateuch" (literally "five utensils," a reference to the cases in which the original scrolls were kept), have traditionally been attributed to Moses. This was due, not to the fact that the books claimed Mosaic authorship, but to the fact that throughout the books his name appears at the beginning of laws or stories. So we read in Exodus 8:1: "Then the LORD said to Moses," or in Numbers 35:9-10: "And the LORD said to Moses, 'Say to the people of Israel.'" In spite of this, the material often bears evidence of having come from later times and sources. In Numbers 31:27, for example, there is a law attributed to Moses about how the booty taken in war was to be distributed. It reads: "Divide the booty into two parts, between the warriors who went out to battle and all the congregation." In 1 Samuel 30:24-25 this same law reappears in slightly different form, and this time it is attributed to David!

All of this tells us that, although Moses may have provided some of the contents of the early part of the Old Testament, much is not from him. Even what may have originally come from Moses has often gone through changes and rephrasing. Thus, scholars have concluded that such expressions as "the Lord said to Moses" or "Moses said" are not indications of authorship, but rather only general formulas to introduce collections of literature. Since Moses was the hero of Israel's early days, and since he had much to do with the establishment of its legal structure, his name has become attached to this material. We are familiar with the same process. An advertisement on television referred to a new edition of the dictionary by the words "as Webster says." Yet we know that the historical Webster wrote none of the definitions in that dictionary. Just as "Webster says" becomes a convenient way to introduce word definitions, "Moses says" was used to introduce legislation, whether or not he actually promulgated it. In 2 Corinthians 3:15 the apostle Paul even uses "Moses" as a designation for the whole Old Testament!

The whole process of selection and arrangement resulted finally in the present grand history of Israel that stretches from creation to reconstruction after the exile. Within this larger scheme are three separate histories, plus two short stories. Each of them has its own theological purpose, and each arose at a different time and from different editors and writers. To the first of them, the Priestly History, we now turn.

PURPOSE OF THE PRIESTLY HISTORY

The Priestly History comprises Genesis, Exodus, Leviticus, and Numbers. Sometime after the destruction of Jerusalem by the Babylonians in 587 B.C., a circle of priests in Jerusalem gathered together some of the older narrative sources, particularly "J" and "E." These were then supplemented by legal and liturgical materials the priests had saved from the destroyed temple. Among these latter texts were some laws in the present book of Leviticus and directions regarding the place of worship (Exodus 25–31 and 35–40). Out of these sources they formed what is called the "Priestly History."

The motive for the formation of this history was Israel's own situation. The community had been destroyed and the people scattered. What could be expected in the future? How should they plan for the future? The priests turned to the past for their guidelines. They sought to show that the world was in the charge of Yahweh, who had called Israel from Egypt to be (1) God's special people in the land of Palestine, and (2) God's missionary people to bring blessing to the whole world. Therefore they taught that Israel had a future because the divine plan, which could not be thwarted, was unfulfilled. They saw that the plan for Israel's existence had been revealed in Genesis 12:1-3 and in the laws of Moses. And so their Priestly History became the foundational document by which the exiles from Babylonian slavery sought to organize themselves.

The heart of this history is the story in Exodus 1–15 of the deliverance by God of Israel from Egypt. This key event, by which the exilic priests interpreted the meaning of history, was the central event to which Israel had looked back for centuries. When an Israelite offered the firstfruits of the harvest to God at a shrine or temple, a prayer was recited in which this deliverance was remembered (Deuteronomy 26:5-10). Exodus 15 itself reflects the remembrance of the Exodus in formal liturgical worship through the years. The prophets often reminded the people of this mighty saving work of God (Amos 2:10; 5:25; 9:7; Hosea 2:15; 11:1; Michah 6:4; Jeremiah 2:6). And at the beginning of the Ten Commandments is a statement about the Egyptian deliverance (Exodus 20:2; Deuteronomy 5:6).

Around this nucleus the rest of the Priestly History took shape. The Exodus from Egypt had demonstrated that Yahweh was sovereign over all the forces and gods of the world and that God had saved Israel for a special relationship. A crucial passage is Exodus 3:7-8. The divine plan for Yahweh's people is spelled out—Israel is promised the land of Canaan. And so quite naturally the account of the deliverance from Egypt is followed by the events that illustrate the unfolding of the plan. The history in Exodus and Numbers traces only events through the wandering in the wilderness. Very probably an account of the conquest and settlement in Palestine originally was placed at the end. The original ending of the narrative has now been lost because it has been replaced by another account of the same event, namely, the Book of Joshua.

The narratives in the book of Genesis seem to have been added as a preface to the history of God's salvation described in Exodus through Numbers. In other words, they are intended not to be simply stories about the primeval days (Genesis 1–11) and patriarchal days (Genesis 12–50), but to be integrally related to the saving acts of God described in the following books. This purpose can be seen in that their interest rests on specifically Israelite concerns. The primeval history stresses not only that it is Yahweh, Israel's God, who is sovereign creator and sustainer of the world, but also that aspects of Israel's life are grounded in that creation. Thus the story of creation comes to its conclusion in the establishment of the sabbath (Genesis 2:3), and the account of the flood includes one of the dietary laws (Genesis 9:4). Although there is much of universal significance in Genesis 1–11, it is intended to be read against the background of the saving plan of God illustrated in Exodus 1–15.

In a similar fashion the patriarchal history of Genesis 12–50 forms a prologue to Exodus 1–15. Separate episodes in the lives of Abraham, Isaac, Jacob, and Joseph are collected and woven together to show how the great salvation from Egypt with its worldwide purpose had been planned from centuries past by Yahweh. These accounts are thus meant to be a justification for Israel and a vindication of Yahweh. What Yahweh had promised to the ancestors of Israel had been fulfilled.

Thus, we read the Priestly History with an eye toward its theological emphasis. It attempts primarily to show us by examples of happenings in the Exodus that history is in the charge of a purposive God who fulfills what is promised. The immediate fulfillment took place in the life of Israel from Abraham to the wilderness wandering. The priests of the exile could draw together these traditions and find meaning for their lives because they believed that God had not changed, that God's purposes had not changed, and that the promises remained to be completely fulfilled. For this same reason and with this same belief, we today read the Priestly History for profit and comfort. Now we must look at this in a little more detail.

THE PRIMEVAL EVENTS (GENESIS 1–11)

The first verse in Genesis says: "In the beginning God created the heavens and the earth." Indeed the name "Genesis" is a transliteration into English of the title of the book in Greek—*geneseos,* "origin, source, beginning." We find the same word at the start of the New Testament in Matthew 1:1: "the book of the genesis [usually translated "generation" or "genealogy," but also "beginning"] of Jesus Christ, the son of David, the son of Abraham." So Genesis is a book of beginnings. But beginnings of what? Of the natural world of rocks and plants and animals and humanity and heavenly bodies? Or of something else? Here it is very important to recognize that Genesis 1–11 deals with the beginnings of the natural world not in order to answer the questions *how* or *when* the world was created. The text sought initially to tell the Israelites *who* created the world, *why* it was created, and *what* part Israel had to play in it. In other words, Genesis 1–11 provides a background to the historical accounts of Israel's life. It sought to show why there was an Israel. There is much that is of universal significance in these accounts. The years of collecting and editing have tended to emphasize those elements in the traditions that are common to all people. So Genesis 1–11 also tells us today *who, why,* and *what.*

The presentation of the material in Genesis 1–11 is given in the form of an extended genealogical list stretching from Adam to Abraham. Its purpose is to show how humanity's basic problems in life are an inevitable development from rebellion against its created relation with God and the world. The authors of the Priestly History brought together various ancient traditions and grouped them around a genealogical list in order to show that with the development of humanity has come the development of problems for humankind. They wanted to show that humanity was created for one purpose by God, but often has done the opposite, and so has reaped destructive results. All of this, then, provides the backdrop to the story of Abraham and of Israel. For starting with Genesis 12:1-3 is the account of God's work in the world to solve humankind's problem through Abraham and his descendants.

1. Creation (1:1–2:25). Genesis begins with two accounts of creation—1:1–2:4*a* and 2:4*b*-25. These are just two perspectives on the same event, each of which makes its own contribution. Actually many other descriptions of creation are scattered throughout the Old Testament. As one looks closely, it becomes clear that in describing these original events the authors were not attempting to be literalistic. They could not know the secrets of how God created, and so they utilized the rich images and figures of speech of their culture to describe that event. Thus if we attempt to ask: "Did it really happen this way?" we are posing the wrong question. A quick look at various passages in the Old Testament will show us how varied were the ways of describing creation. In Genesis 1 God creates *by the spoken word:* "And God said, 'Let there be light'; and there was light." (Notice Psalm 33:6, 9.) In Genesis 2 God creates *by hand:* "Then the LORD God formed man of dust from the ground. . . . And the LORD God planted a garden in Eden." (Compare Genesis 2:7-8 with Psalms 8:3; 104.) Yet again in Isaiah 51:9 God is described as creating *by massive struggle.* (See also Job 26:6-14.) We can see from these few examples that the creation stories in the Bible do not give us a scientific descripton, but a symbolic one. They were trying to present the theological meaning of creation. Here symbol and metaphor communicate meaning far better than does scientific terminology.

With these facts we can understand more clearly the contemporary discussion about whether or not there are "myths" in the Old Testament. If one means by this a sheer fantasy or fiction, then there are no myths in the Old Testament. If one defines a myth as a story about the gods, then the theology of the Old Testament contains no myths. The Israelites produced no myths, because myths in the ancient world were based upon polytheism and magic. To Israel's theologians neither existed. The writers of the Old Testament, however, did borrow motifs and allusions from the myths of Mesopotamia and Canaan as means of describing the significance of God's acts in the world. They never borrowed the mythological materials unchanged, but always transformed them into ways of describing the actions of the one God of the world. We are not unfamiliar with this process. We utilize the imagery of mythology and in the process change the original meaning when we speak of someone "swift as Pegasus" or "strong as Atlas." Thus, Isaiah uses the imagery of the Babylonian myth of creation when he describes the action of the Lord in cutting "Rahab in pieces," in piercing "the dragon" (Isaiah 51:9). In the Babylonian story of creation the world was brought into being when one of the gods slew the sea dragon and cut her in half. Isaiah uses this image as a figure of speech to describe God's creative work on the primordial sea.

Understanding these things helps us in reading the two creation accounts of Genesis. The *first narrative,* Genesis 1:1–2:4*a,* describes creation as a developing process culminating in the formation of humanity. This process, which takes place in six days, is then followed by a day of rest, hallowed by God as a special day set apart. The description of these elements, however, is clearly in terms of the language of an ancient culture. The sky is a solid "firmament" holding back heavenly waters (1:6-8). The ancient threefold botanical division of grass, plants, and seed-bearing trees is used, as well as the threefold cosmological division of sun, moon, and stars, and the threefold classification of land beings as domestic animals, creeping things, and wild animals (1:12, 16, 24). So we do not read this creation story for accurate information about the process of creation. We do not attempt to read eons of time into the word "day." That the story pictures God as resting a day should warn us of the dangers of a too literal interpretation. We read the first creation account for its information about God and humankind.

The story tells us, *first,* that God is sovereign over all of life. In a world where the forces of nature were often the personification of the gods, this concept had special impact. The God of Israel was not part of nature, but sovereign over nature. Everything and everyone was dependent upon God for its existence. *Second,* humanity is different from the rest of creation because it is created "in the image of God." As an image is a "representation" of something, so each person is a representative of God on earth and intended to imitate God's actions. So humanity is commanded to "subdue" the earth (1:28), to have authority over the natural world (1:26, 28), to work with God in bringing order out of disorder, and to share with God in completing the process of creation. One aspect of this imitation of God is the structuring of life around the pattern of a week, and so having a time for work and time for rest and worship. It is to be noted that the description is of "mankind," not of an individual man. This can be seen not only in the term "Adam," which in Hebrew is always a collective term, but also in 1:27: "So God created *man* in his own image, in the image of God he created him; male and female he created *them.*" (Italics are the author's.) That "man" is both male and female stresses both their corporate responsibility to be partners with God and also the close relationship existing between them. Whole "mankind" is male and female.

The *second narrative,* Genesis 2:4*b*-25, views creation as a series of acts beginning with and revolving around humanity. Therefore the focus is different from the first creation account. In chapter 1 the stress is on the process of God's creative activity. Here the emphasis is more on humankind and on the relationships with God and the world that are necessary for humankind to find the significance of life. But again the description of these things is highly picturesque. We read of two trees in the Garden of Eden, one to give life and the other to give the knowledge of good and evil (2:9). From the first tree the man and the woman were allowed to eat, but not from the second (2:16-17). The reason for the prohibition we shall note in a moment. We also read of the formation of man from the "dust" of the ground (2:7) and of woman from a "rib" taken from the man (2:22). Furthermore, the order of creation is different from that in chapter 1. Here man is formed first, not last, and then everything else is created in relation to man—plants for food and life (2:8-9), animals for help (2:18-20), and woman for companionship and sexual fulfillment (2:21-24). Humankind is depicted here as originally vegetarian; not until after the rebellion against God was the eating of meat allowed (9:2-6). Here is a reminder that there is something wrong and unnatural about killing, even of animals.

This account of creation tells us, *first,* that humankind has been created to be controlled by God and is dependent upon God for its origin (2:7), for its continuing life (2:9), and for its pattern of life (2:15-17). Humankind was created to live in a place of bliss and to find fulfillment only when recognizing its responsibilities to

God. Rejection of dependence upon God inevitably means disaster, because humankind has been created to find fulfillment only in this way. *Second,* the account says that humankind has been made to control the world and is commanded to subdue the natural order (2:15) and the animal order (2:19-20). Humankind is not to seek to escape from the world, but to utilize it constructively for the purposes of God and for its own enjoyment. Work, possessions, sexual relationships, natural enjoyments are all good things if motivated by divine concerns. *Third,* the story tells us that humankind was created to share control. This is illustrated in the relationship between male and female and in the expression "it is not good that man should be alone" (2:18). With the creation of woman the man now has a "helper fit for him." The word "fit" means literally "answering" or "corresponding" to him. We stand in need of sharing life with others. This is true in the sexual life and in all areas of life. This is epitomized in Leviticus 19:18: "You shall love your neighbor as yourself."

2. The Garden of Eden (Genesis 3:1-24). Chapter 3 is really a continuation of the story begun at 2:4*b* and so continues the same use of imagery. It is still the same story of all men and women, not just an original pair. Humankind is personified by a husband and wife. They are put in a garden called "Eden" (delight, paradise), where they are allowed all its enjoyments except for the fruit of "the tree of the knowledge of good and evil." The creative intention of God, as we saw, was for humankind to be in a good world, free to enjoy it, but not free from restrictions or commands. Yet we who read this account know that our world is not an Eden. There is much enjoyment and beauty, to be sure; but there is also much pain and hate and hardship. Why? Chapter 3 gives the answer.

The loss of Eden is due to humankind's rebellion against what it was created to be and do. Humankind has misused its freedom and rebelled against a dependent, obedient relationship to God, as depicted by the incident of the serpent and the eating of the fruit. The serpent was an especially appropriate symbol, for, in the culture from which this account came, the serpent was a personification of various gods and goddesses and particularly connected with wisdom and fertility powers. Here there is no mythology; the serpent is another creature, albeit a special creature, created by God: "Now the serpent was more subtle than any other wild creature that the LORD God had made" (3:1). In the story the serpent tempts the woman to disobey God and to eat from the tree of knowledge. It promises freedom and independence and suggests that God is unfair to keep humans from all the trees of the garden. In fact, it says, God is jealous and selfish, "for God knows that when you eat of it your eyes will be opened, and you will be like God, knowing good and evil" (3:5). The serpent symbolizes the eternal temptation—to rebel against God and serve other gods. Man and woman eat and find hardship, tragedy, and death. The serpent had lied. People's true freedom and fulfillment only come by accepting their positions as creatures dependent upon God.

The story tells us that "sin" in its most basic sense is humanity's movement away from dependence upon God. It also tells us that the inevitable result is disaster. So "sin" is any act that is destructive to the wholeness and well-being of self, family, or larger group, since it is rebellion against God's way of finding fulfillment as a created being. Sin may take many forms—indifference, pride, indolence, immorality, murder, and so on—but there is only one root, namely, rebellion against God. This is the meaning of the expression "the knowledge of good and evil." In the Old Testament this is an idiom for "everything" (Genesis 24:50), and then for "adulthood" or "maturity" (Deuteronomy 1:39; Isaiah 7:15). One who "knows good and evil" is an adult. In the symbolism of the story we are told that humankind was formed to live obedient to God in childlike dependence. Humanity's sin is its move toward independence and autonomy symbolized by adulthood.

3. The Progress of Sin (Genesis 4:1–11:32). The rest of the primeval history is concerned to show the results of the marred relationship between God and humankind. It is a series of old traditions selected to illustrate typical ways that human life has been disturbed and destroyed because of sin. Built on a genealogical structure, these traditions depict the character of life that inevitably develops outside Eden and show that one can trace humanity's problems back to the rebellion against God.

It is very important to keep in mind that we are still reading picturesque literature. In answer to the question, Did it happen exactly this way? we must answer no! This is parabolic literature, not historical literature. The growth of civilization, for example, depicted in chapter 4 is patently nonhistorical. It says in 4:17 that Cain was the founder of urban or city life, but not until later did nomadic or bedouin life arise (4:20). This sequence contradicts not only 4:2, but also the abundant evidence of anthropology that nomadic existence was anterior to urban life. So we read these chapters similarly to the way we read Jesus' parable of the rich man and Lazarus (Luke 16:19-31). These are accounts that deal with the realities of life, but not always in literalistic ways.

The progress of sin begins with the story of the two brothers (Genesis 4:1-26). Here are represented typical effects of rebellion against God—jealousy, murder, and a sneering attitude. Cain then moves away from his family and inaugurates the main elements in culture (4:17-22). Here, too, sin rears its head in that this advancement brings increasing social animosities. Thus sin brings not only murder, but also repeated murder, for Lamech boasts of an unremitting blood revenge. The next major illustration of sin's effects occurs in the prologue to the Flood. This is the story of angels mingling with women and producing giant offspring (6:1-4). The account then tells us that superhuman evil has infested the human race. The language is borrowed from mythology, but the truth is taken from reality. There is a demonic power among humankind.

The Flood story (6:5–9:17) reminds us that sweeping judgments come upon humanity's rebellious, demonic life. (Notice 6:5-7.) But again this is described by the use of popular imagery. The Flood story is not a reporter's description of an historical event. It is based on an old tradition, familiar in the ancient world, about a great, destructive flood. Here the legend has been expanded into a universal flood. But whether or not there was a local or universal flood is not important. What is important is the meaning. In the pagan accounts the gods sent a flood to exterminate humankind for irresponsible reasons. In one account humankind made so much noise that the gods could not sleep. But in Genesis the Flood comes as a just divine judgment on human wickedness. The story is attempting to stress that evil brings widespread death and destruction. This is a simple point, amply illustrated throughout history. Humanity's demonic nature preys on other people, and widespread destruction results. Yet the story also shows us that God does not forget humanity even in the midst of death and destruction. Chapter 9:1-17 shows God renewing the original creation command for humankind to take an active part in life. The rainbow (9:12-17) becomes a comforting sign that God is not through with humankind even in the midst of its wickedness.

The final episode in the progress of sin is the account of the tower of Babel (11:1-9). The building of a "ziggurat" or great temple in Mesopotamia depicts humankind's attempt to manipulate its own security by establishing an indestructible "name" or reputation. (Notice 11:4.) Humankind seeks to order its own life on its own terms; it is still in rebellion against dependence upon God. But the account shows in the confusion of languages and scattering of the populace another result of rejecting God. Human relationships become disturbed, and people are unable to communicate with one another. Mutual misunderstanding and inability to get along together take place.

THE PATRIARCHAL EVENTS (GENESIS 12–50)

The stories in Genesis 12–50 contain the second part of the introduction to the history of Israel that begins in the book of Exodus. The primeval history of Genesis 1–11 had set the stage by showing God's purpose for humankind but concluded with the evidence that humankind had not achieved this and instead had become murderous, fragmented, and dispersed. The divine plan seemed to have gone awry. But Genesis 12–50 tells us not to judge the evidence too quickly. God is not finished with humankind. And so the patriarchal history begins with a sweeping promise to a man called Abram (later named Abraham): "By you all the families of the earth will be blessed" (12:3). And so begins another step in God's creative work in the world.

Genesis 12–50 is simply the story of three successive generations of a family of Semites, the descendants of Shem, who had migrated into Canaan from Mesopotamia (11:10-32). This is an important family, for its members were the ancestors of the Israelites. These stories provide a link in the chain that leads from creation to Israel. This link, however, is important for more than its genealogical information. It tells us that what God began to do in the formation of Israel had been prepared centuries before. Israel's existence was all part of a deliberate divine plan that stretched back to creation. This is why the patriarchal history is interlaced with the promises of God that Abraham's descendants would bring blessing to the whole world. When Israel came into being, its growth was simply the outworking of this ancient plan.

There are three cycles or clusters of stories in the patriarchal history. These revolve around Abraham, Jacob, and Joseph. Isaac is also mentioned and perhaps originally had his own cycle of stories, but in this collection he is a minor character. These patriarchs are depicted largely as seminomads, wandering from area to area in Canaan searching for grazing land and markets for cattle. Joseph is an exception to this, for he is taken to Egypt and there becomes an official in the royal court. Many in the past have thought that these stories were generally the fabrication of later generations of Israelites. One of the reasons for this was the belief that reliable history had to be written on the basis of contemporary records. The patriarchal events took place between the twentieth and the sixteenth centuries B.C., but the sources used to write the patriarchal history date between the ninth and the sixth centuries B.C. Even if Moses (fourteenth to thirteenth centuries B.C.) had written them, he would have done so centuries after the events. Another reason was that there was very little extra-biblical evidence for the patriarchal period. One could not tell, therefore, if the stories had preserved accurate accounts of events and places and customs. So it was believed that the patriarchs were largely mythical figures, prototypes of ideal Israelites.

Today the situation has changed, although there is still no piece of evidence that specifically mentions the biblical characters. On the one hand, it is becoming increasingly recognized that oral tradition may preserve traditions with extreme accuracy. Even though the sources are much later, this does not mean their contents are historically suspect. And, on the other hand, archaeological discoveries have now illuminated this period in history. Tens of thousands of inscriptions have come to light giving a record of political, business, and family affairs. They show that the movements and customs of the patriarchs fit exactly into the age from which they claim to have come. We now know, for example, that during the patriarchal period large groups of people had migrated into Canaan from the East in search of cultivatable land. Abraham's descent into Palestine would be a small part of this movement. We also know that certain customs were in evidence during the patriarchal period. It was common, for example, for a barren wife to give a slave woman to her husband in order to have a child. This same practice is described in Genesis 16. All of this, of course, does not prove that the patriarchal stories happened as the text says. It neither proves that God was involved nor that there were actual men called Abraham, Jacob, or Joseph. But it does show how firmly rooted in historical reality are the stories.

The world in which the patriarchs moved was composed of cultures that believed rather consistently in the existence of many gods and goddesses. Biblical and archaeological evidence has given us the names of many of these—El, Baal, Elyon, Chemosh, and so on. There is nothing in the patriarchal history to suggest that the patriarchs believed any differently. There is no struggle with idolatry such as we discover later in the Old Testament. And there are textual statements that give us clues as to the situation. The First Commandment states: "You shall have no other gods *beside* me" (Exodus 20:3, italics are the author's). The command does not say that there are no other gods, but only that the God of Israel demands exclusive loyalty. Similarly, in Joshua 24:2 it is stated that the ancestors of the Israelites worshiped "other gods," and in verses 14-18 Joshua charges his people to "put away" these gods and to serve only the Lord.

So the patriarchs were not monotheists; that is, they did not believe in the existence of only one God. Yet they were not polytheists; they did not worship many gods. While assuming the existence of various gods and goddesses, they apparently worshiped only one, whom they gave various names (Genesis 14:20; 17:1; 21:33; 31:42; 49:24). Each generation perhaps had its own special terminology for God. The move towards monotheism really began with Moses but came to its clearest expression in the Book of Isaiah (44:6, 8; 45:5-6). So what the text shows is that before the Israelites came to understand that there was only one God in existence, they first had to learn to be loyal to one God in the midst of competing loyalties. The distinctiveness of patriarchal faith does not really lie here; others expressed loyalty to a tribal or national god. What is unique about the God of the patriarchs is the fact that this God enters into personal relationships with them and shows loving care for all people. There was no god like this in Canaan, Egypt, or Mesopotamia.

There are two clues that are helpful in understanding the patriarchal narratives. The first is found in the *patriarchal promise.* Genesis 12 begins with a call by God to Abram/Abraham to leave his home and journey to an unknown land. This call is followed by a tremendous promise that if Abram would respond, God would bless him with numerous descendants, who would become a great nation and a great blessing to the whole world (12:1-3). In response to this, Abram travels to the land of Canaan. And as he wanders here and there, and his descendants take up the story and have the promise repeated to them (26:4; 28:14), we see the point constantly being made. God promised something; nothing is going to stand in the way of God's fulfillment of that promise. The patriarchal stories have been collected as illustrations of this fact.

The second clue can be seen in the *patriarchal covenant.* This takes place in two parts. In Genesis 15:7-21 God reiterates the promise to Abram and then seals it by a strange ceremony. One of the ways of confirming agreements or covenants in that period was for both parties to pass together between the severed parts of a sacrificial animal. The implication of this action was that in failing to honor the agreement, one would then be calling a similar fate on oneself. (Notice Jeremiah 34:18.) But here there is an important change. God alone (symbolized by the "smoking fire pot" and "flaming torch," 15:17) passes through the pieces. This is meant to stress that God alone is able to bring the promise to fulfillment. Humanity is to have its part, but God alone is the covenant fulfiller.

In Genesis 17:1-27 the covenant is expanded by the rite of circumcision. Repeating the promise to Abram (now Abraham), God commands him to circumcise every male as a "sign" of the covenant (17:11). The emphasis is still the same; it is God alone who gives the promise. But now a means in keeping with ancient culture has been provided by which humankind may show outwardly that it has accepted by faith this promise of God. Each of the patriarchal cycles of stories will emphasize an aspect of this promise and covenant.

1. The Abraham Stories (Genesis 12:1–25:18). This first cycle of stories is concerned largely with the struggle over *the beginning of the divine promise.* These accounts do not really present a connected narrative, but are a collection of somewhat unrelated episodes in the life of Abraham. Yet there is a common theme, and it centers upon Isaac. Isaac appears, not so much as an individual in his own right, but as the point around which the incidents in Abraham's life have been grouped. The birth of Isaac (21:1-7) is intended to be the foil for Abraham's struggle with the fulfillment of promise. The cycle opens, as we saw, with the great promise of descendants, reputation, and blessing (12:1-3). The narratives before the birth of Isaac show Abraham's response to frustrating delays in fulfillment. After Isaac's birth the accounts stress Abraham's struggle with Isaac's real ability to fulfill the promise. There are, of course, other secondary elements in the stories, for more than one factor has entered into the gathering of traditions. But through all the accounts there is an underlying affirmation: History is in the charge of a purposive God. People may delay the divine promises, but they cannot ultimately thwart them.

This dominant theme is graphically depicted. On the one hand, the patriarch is shown as a man unable to believe. We see this in his attempt to save his life by passing off Sarah to the pharaoh (12:10-20) and to Abimelech (20:1-18) as his sister. By his own attempt at shrewdness, he almost thwarts the fulfillment of the promise. Sarah is apparently lost in the harem until Yahweh intercedes. In the time of crisis Abraham is unable to believe God's promises. Again, in the incident of Hagar (16:1-16), fearful that Sarah was barren and that the promise could not be fulfilled, Abraham followed the custom of his day and had a child by Sarah's Egyptian maid Hagar. He attempted to provide his own fulfillment. Again Yahweh had to show the true fulfillment.

On the other hand, Abraham is often shown to be a man of faith. His faith led him to leave familiar surroundings and journey to an unknown land (12:4-9). In Abraham's struggle with Lot over grazing rights, the patriarch allowed Lot to choose the better land in the faith that God would not abandon him (13:1-18). In the Melchizedek story he gave eloquent testimony to his belief that "the LORD God Most High, maker of heaven and earth" was the true mover in the affairs of humanity (14:1-23). And in his willingness to offer Isaac as a sacrifice to God, the ultimate example of Abraham's faith is shown (22:1-19). It is this kind of trust that lies behind the basic statement in 15:6: "And he believed the LORD; and he reckoned it to him as righteousness." Abraham became a partner in fulfillment.

2. The Jacob Stories (Genesis 25:19–36:43). The second cycle of patriarchal narratives deals with the struggle over *the inheritance of the divine promise.* Isaac had begun the fulfillment of promise. But Isaac had more than one son. Who was to carry on the promise? Who was to receive the blessings of fulfillment? Who was to be the patriarch? The stories in this cycle attempt to show the conflict between Jacob and Esau over the inheritance of this blessing and leadership.

The Jacob stories provide a variety of important facts. Not only do they give cultural and political information, but their primary emphasis is on theological meaning. On the one hand, they show us how open-eyed were the biblical writers to the realities of life. They do not idealize their ancestors. Abraham is depicted in his unfaith, and Jacob is shown in his unscrupulousness. For his whole life Jacob was a cheat. He fooled his father; he duped his brother, and he tricked his father-in-law. Yet this man was the father of the Israelite people! The stories of Jacob have to be seen, on the other hand, against the theological theme of all the patriarchal stories. The fulfillment of God's promises ultimately does not rest on human merit and achievement, but on divine grace and power. This truth is epitomized in Jacob's dream of the ladder from heaven (27:46–28:22). Forced to leave home because of Esau's wrath, Jacob spends the night at Bethel. In a dream he sees a ladder reaching from earth to heaven with angels ascending and descending on it. At its top the Lord stands and renews the covenant promise to Jacob. In response Jacob gives a vow of faithful obedience (28:20-21) that is meant to be the motto of all God's people. The story affirms that God will not let humankind's weakness and deviousness cause the promise to fail. God will even use a rogue like Jacob to provide salvation for humankind.

3. The Joseph Stories (Genesis 37:1–50:26). The third cycle of patriarchal stories is concerned with the struggle over *the continuance of the divine promise.* In the process this series provides the necessary introduction to the story of Israel. It shows us how the Israelites came to be in Egypt. Jacob, whose other name was Israel (32:27-28), had twelve sons. Because of family conflict, one of them named Joseph was sold by his brothers to traders who took him to Egypt. There he rose to power as an administrator to the pharaoh. During a severe famine in Canaan the family of Jacob came to Egypt looking for grain. There they were reunited with Joseph and settled down to live. The story ends with Joseph's death, and the stage is now set for the next act which begins in the book of Exodus.

This remarkable story is a fascinating example of the richness of Old Testament literature. The biblical traditions have preserved many ways of presenting their message, sometimes through rather sober history, sometimes through genealogical lists. Here it is through a folktale, that is, an entertaining story. All deal with reality, but each deals in its own way. The account of Joseph's life is basically not a history, but a novel. This does not mean that it is fabrication. It only means we must learn to appreciate the storyteller's art and to read it with an eye toward the message. This message is clearly in a line with that of the Abraham and Jacob cycles—in and through all of life, God is at work. Joseph claims as much in his last words to his brothers: "As for you, you meant evil against me; but God meant it for good" (Genesis 50:20). In each episode in Joseph's life this fact is made clear. Thrown by his brothers into a pit without water, doomed to die and bring the promise to an end, Joseph is miraculously rescued out of the pit and sold to some traders (37:12-28). Sold into slavery in Egypt, Joseph is providentially purchased by a man who is willing to allow him to develop his abilities. And by this, a chain of events is begun that eventually leads Joseph to a position of leadership in the nation. All of these events bear the mark of God's sovereignty, for by them Abraham's descendants are preserved, and the promise is able to continue.

THE SALVATION EVENTS (EXODUS–NUMBERS)

With the book of Exodus the central part of the Priestly History has been reached. We now read the story of God's deliverance of the descendants of Abraham from Egyptian slavery and of their formation into a people called "Israel." As we saw, the material in the book of Genesis has been preparatory for this. The primeval and patriarchal histories have given us the reason why the calling of Israel was necessary and have shown us how the descendants of Abraham got into Egypt.

1. Deliverance from Egypt (Exodus 1–18). The close of the book of Genesis has described how Jacob and his family had gone to Egypt to escape the famine in Canaan. Crops were more dependable in Egypt than in Canaan because of the annual overflow of the Nile. So it was not unusual for tribes to come to Egypt during periods of drought. (Notice Genesis 12 and 26.) At first the Egyptians had received the Hebrews favorably because of the influence of Joseph. But in the opening chapter of Exodus a change has taken place. Some time has passed, and Joseph and his generation have died. A new pharaoh has come to power, and now the Hebrews are made slaves of the Egyptians. So chapters 2–14 describe the calling of Moses by God to be the deliverer of the enslaved Hebrews and how, by means of a series of plagues (7–11) and a miraculous crossing of the Red Sea (12–14), this deliverance is achieved. This is followed by a song of praise to God from those who have been delivered (15). The section concludes with an account of God's further care for the people as they wander in the wilderness of Sinai (15–18).

There is no record apart from the Bible that directly substantiates these events, nor that establishes the period in which they happened. We have already seen that a humiliating defeat of an Egyptian army was not the kind of thing that appeared in official Egyptian records. There is, however, some indirect evidence which does not prove the biblical account but at least shows its great possibility. *First,* there are various Egyptian inscriptional and artistic materials from this period that give evidence that Semites from Sinai and Palestine were allowed to enter Egypt and settle on its borders. *Second,* there are Israelite names in the biblical account that have an Egyptian background. These can be found particularly in the tribe of Levi, such as Hophni, Phinehas, Merari. Even the name Moses is from the Egyptian verb "to beget." This verb is often found in the names of pharaohs to suggest that a certain god had begotten the king. Thus one finds "Thutmosis," that is, "begotten by the god Thur"; another one is "Raamses" or "begotten by the god Ra." *Third,* we are told in Exodus 1:11 that the Egyptian king made the Hebrew slaves build two cities, Pithom and Raamses. Since these cities can be identified in the Nile delta region, the context suggests that the time was around 1300 B.C. The capital had been at Thebes in Upper Egypt, but shortly after 1300 B.C. Pharaoh Raamses II moved it to the delta area. *Fourth,* the account of the Exodus is not the kind of tradition a people would invent. At the heart of it is the claim that God chose them, not because of special merit, but because of love. Here were a people who did not come into prominence because of military prowess, but because God had delivered them from slavery.

In the faith of Israel, as we saw, the Exodus was central. This was the moment of Israel's beginning and therefore the event that gave meaning to its whole existence. In the memory of Israel it was not just a historical event; it was the time when God had called the people for a special role and life. Thus the Passover festival became the most important moment in Jewish worship for understanding their vocation and destiny. Similar to the Lord's Supper in Christian worship, the Passover was the central act of worship in Jewish practice. So when succeeding generations observed the remembrance of this event, they were intended to see themselves as part of the delivered and called group. The occasion spelled out their vocation, as well as that of the first generation. We see this, for example, in the liturgical formula for offering the firstfruits: "The Egyptians treated *us* harshly, and afflicted *us,* and laid upon *us* hard bondage. Then . . . the LORD brought *us* out of Egypt" (Deuteronomy 26:6, 8; italics are the author's). For this reason some scholars feel that the present form of the Passover and Exodus narrative found in Exodus 1–15 can best be explained as due to the fact that it was written down following centuries of use in the liturgy of Israel. Thus the narrative reflects the language and concerns of worship, rather than of history. In other words, when the writer of Exodus 1–15 came to preserve the story, the source material was largely that which had been used for recitation in public worship. This is why there appear throughout the story some worship elements that obviously were not part of the original event. The night on which the Passover lamb was killed is described in 12:42 in a way that shows the writer's knowledge of its repeated observance among successive generations. This is also why chapter 15 is a song of praise to Yahweh for the deliverance from Egypt (15:1-12) as well as a victory hymn glorifying the royal temple in Jerusalem where the Passover feast was held (15:13-18).

All of this helps us to read Exodus 1–18 with greater understanding. The purpose of the historical narrative is primarily to glorify the God of Israel. This, of course, fits it into the whole theological motivation of the Priestly History. The story attempts to show us that all nature, all gods, and all people are in the hands of Yahweh, the God of Israel. We learn of real events, but we learn about them in a way that shows us that it was because Yahweh is sovereign over all forces that the escape was possible. This note strikes us at the beginning of the story. The people of Israel are groaning under their bondage, "and God heard their groaning, and God remembered his covenant with Abraham, with Isaac, and with Jacob" (Exodus 2:24). God had promised something a long time ago; nothing was going to stand in the way of the fulfillment of that promise. The rest of the narrative flows out of this. God appears to Moses and says, "I have seen the affliction of my people who are in Egypt . . . and I have come down to deliver them out of the hand of the Egyptians" (Exodus 3:7-8). So in the actual confrontation with the pharaoh, the dominant motif is not the personal struggle between Moses and the Egyptian king, but between Yahweh, the God of Israel, and the gods of Egypt. Thus all through the account are laced the claims of Yahweh's absolute control. Again and again it is claimed that the king was under God's control (for example, 7:3; 14:18), or that nature was dominated by God (for example 9:29; 14:21), or that the gods of Egypt could not resist Israel's God (for example, 12:12; 15:11). Hence, the final song of praise appropriately begins: "I will sing to the LORD, for he has triumphed gloriously."

We must remember this when we read the description of the magical acts of Moses (4), or the account of the plagues (7–11), or the crossing of the great sea (14–15), or the miracles of quail, manna, water, and victory over the Amalekites (16–17). These are written with liturgical and theological interests dominant; thus the accounts have been shaped to highlight the power of God. There is bound to be overstatement or poetic exaggeration of events. This does not mean that the basic events did not happen. If God is truly sovereign over this world, as the stories repeatedly affirm, then one cannot exclude God from it. Yet we have to realize that the events did not always happen exactly as they are recorded. The crossing of the Red Sea is a good example. This, by the way, was not a crossing of what is today called the Red Sea. The Hebrew is literally the "Reed Sea," and the Red Sea has no reeds. Where this body of water was no one knows. It was probably one of the lakes in lower Egypt that today are connected by the Suez canal. What actually took place when the Israelites crossed is difficult to say. Exodus 14:21-22 says that the Lord drove the sea back by a strong east wind, so that the water stood up like walls on both sides of a path. It was dry land to the Israelites, but when the Egyptians tried to follow, they became clogged in the muddy bottom and drowned when the waters returned. This event has been given an imaginative reporting in chapter 15. The water was forced back by a blast from the nostrils of Yahweh (15:8), who then cast the Egyptians into the sea (15:4). When one reads this passage, various questions arise. If the wind was so strong, how could the Israelites have crossed? If the Egyptians' chariots became clogged, what prevented the same thing happening to the Israelites? The narratives do not answer these questions, nor are they intended to do so. They wished, above all, to make clear that "the LORD saved Israel that day from the hand of the Egyptians; and Israel saw the Egyptians dead upon the seashore" (14:30).

2. Encounter at Mount Sinai (Exodus 19:1–Numbers 10:10). Three months after the Israelites escaped from Egypt, they arrived at Mount Sinai (Exodus 19:1). Here they were to stay for about eleven months before moving off towards Canaan (Numbers 10:11-12). But during this brief period they encountered and entered into covenant with God, and received the laws by which this bond of communion was to be maintained and Israel's life was to be conducted. As with the rest of the historical and legal materials, however, the form in which we now have the story is the result of centuries of transmission and use. There are various elements in the story that come from much later periods of time than the actual encounter by the fleeing Israelites with God at Mount Sinai.

a. *The covenant with Yahweh* (Exodus 19:1–24:18). We learn first that Moses climbed Mount Sinai and heard God telling him to prepare the people to enter into a covenant (19:1-25). This account is followed by a listing of the fundamental laws of the covenant, namely, the Decalogue (Exodus 20:1-17). Exodus 20: 22–23:33 contains, for the most part, a collection of legislation from the later period of the judges that seeks to apply the fundamental law to specific situations. Exodus 24:1-18 provides the conclusion, telling of a covenant meal eaten by Moses and the seventy elders on the mountain in the presence of God. There are various things of importance here.

(1) *Relationship to Abraham.* The covenant established with Israel at Mount Sinai was not a separate covenant distinct from the relationship with Abraham. The promise had been given to Abraham (Genesis 12:1-3), and the covenant had been made in the strange ceremony of the pieces (Genesis 15). Now at Mount Sinai we see a reaffirmation and partial fulfillment of the convenantal promises. Exodus 2:24 tells us that the motivation for the deliverance from Egypt was God's remembrance of this covenant with Abraham, Isaac, and Jacob. (Notice Deuteronomy 7:6-8; Jeremiah 11:1-5.) What was unique about the event at Mount Sinai was that it was the next step in fulfillment; it was the time of the establishment of Israel as a distinct people with their own laws and organization. This is the meaning of Yahweh's words by which Israel was called to be "a kingdom of priests and a holy nation" (Exodus 19:4-6). Israel was a kingdom of mediators ("priests") between God and the world, a nation set apart ("holy") for the worldwide service of the Lord. In other words, here Israel is given the choice ("if you will obey my voice and keep my covenant") of being used as the instrument in fulfilling God's worldwide concerns. The covenant required human participation for its fulfillment.

This concept of the covenant is simply that although the fulfillment of God's purposes for the world is guaranteed, the manner and time of their fulfillment are partially conditioned by human response. This is another way of illustrating God's concern to work through humankind to fulfill these divine purposes, as in the creation of humans in "God's image," to be partners or representatives of God. So Israel was to be the partner of God. Failure to respond, as it happened, would cost Israel this special role. But the promise would still be fulfilled, even though by other means. Thus, the church in the New Testament interprets its role as the new means of fulfilling God's purpose.

(2) *Regulations for response.* The covenant regulations are contained in two collections. There are two basic legal formulations collected in this context. The *first* is the Decalogue or "Ten Words" in Exodus 20:2-17. This contains the original covenant regulations, although in its present form it reflects some later additions. The table of laws occurs again in Deuteronomy 5:6-21 but in slightly different form. Most striking is the difference in reason for keeping the sabbath. Both forms begin with the statement: "I am the LORD your God, who brought you out of the land of Egypt, out of the house of bondage." This affirmation sets the law in the context of grace and stresses that obedience to law is to be seen against the background of grateful response and release to freedom. In other words, law was intended to be received not as a burden but as a gift of life. Its regulations were intended by God to provide the way for Israel to find freedom; they were part of the whole event of release from slavery. So the Hebrew word "law" conveys the ideas of "guidance, teaching, training." (Notice Proverbs 1:8; 3:1; 7:2; Job 22:22.) The *second* collection of laws is the Covenant Code found in Exodus 20:22–23:33. It gets its name from its present place in the text in relation to the covenant meal and the reading of the "book of the covenant" (24:7). In that context the term would seem to refer to the preceding laws, namely, the Decalogue and the Covenant Code. But the Covenant Code actually developed at a time later than Mount Sinai. It springs from the period of the judges, that is, shortly after the conquest of Canaan. It deals with the legal problems of that period, namely, with the life of an agricultural people. There is no mention of a king and very little with regard to urban life. This collection

of later laws was placed here as part of the revelation on Mount Sinai for a very good reason. The Decalogue by itself cannot be a code by which people can regulate their lives. It is too general. It must be applied specifically to various areas of life. The Covenant Code was placed here, even though it contains laws from various periods, as an illustration of how the Decalogue was interpreted in the various situations in the life of early Israel, and perhaps to teach Israel that each generation had the right and responsibility to apply the fundamental policies of the Decalogue in ways that were fitting to their situation.

b. *The Priestly Code* (Exodus 25:1–Numbers 10:10). The rest of the materials dealing with the encounter at Mount Sinai may be called the Priestly Code. This is a vast collection that gathers together the cultic legislation of Israel. It is in two forms: narrative, describing how the laws originated; and legal, giving the various commands. Again we must recognize, as with the Covenant Code, that most of the laws in the Priestly Code did not originate at Mount Sinai. These come from all periods of Israel's history. They have been inserted here to identify them as providing the will of Yahweh for the cultic or formal religious area of life. Thus with the Decalogue, Covenant Code, and Priestly Code we are given God's law for life. The Decalogue provides the basic mandates for divine and human relationships. But these are too general and need explanation. The Covenant Code shows what they mean for daily life, while the Priestly Code explains the meaning for cultic life. There is another Code which also deals primarily with daily life, namely, the Deuteronomic Code. We will look at this later.

(1) *The tabernacle and priesthood* (Exodus 25:1–40:38). The first section in the Priestly Code contains the directions for building, staffing, and operating the center of worship. Moses is described as receiving from the Lord the details of the tabernacle (place of dwelling), its furniture, and its priestly staff (25–31). These laws are then interrupted by a series of episodes dealing with the people's impatience with Moses because of his long stay on the mount receiving the Laws from the Lord (32–34). Because people were anxious to get moving toward Canaan, they chose another leader, Aaron, and persuaded him to make them a golden bull. This image was intended to symbolize the presence of a god who

would lead them across the wilderness. But Moses returned from the mount, discovered the rebellion, and smashed the stone tablets upon which the Law was written. He then melted down the image and slaughtered a great number of the Israelites. Others were killed by a plague. God then provided help for the people's forthcoming journey across the unknown wilderness, replaced the broken tablets of the Law, and renewed the covenant by giving another set of laws. The whole section concludes with a narrative description of the actual building and staffing of the tabernacle (35–40). This is a virtual repetition of the material in chapters 25–31.

(a) *Tabernacle.* The purpose of the tabernacle is given in Exodus 25:8: "And let them make me a sanctuary, that I may dwell in their midst." The various names used to describe it all reflect this purpose. It is called a "sanctuary," that is, "a place set apart for God." In Exodus 25:9 it is termed a "tabernacle" or "a place of dwelling." In Exodus 33:7 it is a "tent of meeting." Thus, although the Old Testament recognizes that God cannot be localized, it also understands that God can be manifest in various places. The tabernacle provided the focal point for this manifestation and a visible structure around which to organize worship and from which to receive revelation. It tended to remind Israel that all of life was Yahweh-centered. Each of the pieces of furniture in the tabernacle—the altar of burnt offering, the laver, the table of showbread, the golden candlestick, the altar of incense, and the ark of the covenant—as well as the directions regarding which persons could utilize them, was intended to provide instruction in the meaning of worship. The fact that the tabernacle was primarily the place of God's presence provides the background to the New Testament doctrine of Incarnation. Jesus Christ the Word "dwelt [literally 'tabernacled'] among us" (John 1:14) and was the one in whom "all the fulness of God was pleased to dwell" (Colossians 1:19).

(b) *Priesthood.* The whole nation of Israel was intended to be a "kingdom of priests" (Exodus 19:6), yet within it there were those set apart as representatives of all the people who conducted the formal worship. This division was partly for practical reasons; it would have been virtually impossible for everyone to offer sacrifices at the tabernacle or temple. So their representative did. But it was also for spiritual reasons. The people as a whole needed constant reminders of their special role, as well as instruction from God regarding the various problems of life. The function of the priesthood was to represent the people before God and to represent God before the people.

The priesthood had a threefold hierarchy. At the head was the high priest who not only gave general oversight and instruction, but also was the one who led the worship on special days, particularly on the Day of Atonement (Leviticus 16). The next order were the priests. Their duties at the tabernacle or temple were to care for the worship, including the offering of sacrifices (Numbers 18:5, 7). Outside the place of worship they had varied duties of teaching the law (Leviticus 10–11; Malachi 2:6-7), administering justice (Deuteronomy 17:8-12), and safeguarding the health and purity of the people (Leviticus 13–15). The lowest in order were the Levites. Their function was to assist the priests in the menial duties of the sanctuary (Numbers 1:50; 3:6, 8; 16:9). Some of them also assisted as musicians (Ezra 3:10; Nehemiah 12:27).

(2) *The laws regarding worship* (Leviticus 1:1–27:34). The last part of Exodus described the structure of tabernacle and priesthood, and now quite logically comes a collection of laws concerning worship in that tabernacle where the priesthood would minister. One collection is called the "Holiness Code" (Leviticus 17:1–26:46), a name that is derived from the frequently recurring admonition: "You shall be holy; for I the LORD your God am holy" (19:1; 20:7, 26; 21:6). The word "holy" means "to be set apart to God's realm," and thus the laws deal with God's concern in Israel's cultic and ethical life. Although most of the laws deal with public worship, one of the greatest statements of the Old Testament is found in its midst: "You shall love your neighbor as yourself: I am the LORD" (19:18).

(a) *Sacrifices.* We have already encountered mention of sacrifices in previous passages (for example, Exodus 20:24; 24:5), but here we have the first summary of the regulations regarding these sacrifices. The very fact that we find the practice of sacrifice described before the regulations for sacrifice are given is illustrative again of the composite nature of these materials. We do not read in our present texts a chronological report of events. We read in Leviticus an anthology of materials clustered around theological themes or events comprising traditions spanning religious practice over a thousand years of Israel's history. Hence, it is extremely difficult to know what parts of the sacrificial laws were observed and in force during the different periods in Israel's life. The sacrificial laws we now read in Leviticus 1–7 represent the fully developed practice of the Jerusalem temple in postexilic days. Some of them stem back to Mosaic times, but others do not, so it is not possible to harmonize all the details. It is stated, for example, that for the burnt offering the offerer is to kill the animal (Leviticus 1:5), to skin it, cut it in pieces, and wash the entrails and feet (Leviticus 1:6, 9). But Ezekiel 44:11 states that the Levites did the killing, and 2 Chronicles 29:22, 24, 34 claim the priests were the ones required to kill the animal and cut up its parts. This is simply an illustration that sacrificial practice developed through the years and was not always the same. A surface reading of Leviticus 1–7 might lead one to a false conclusion.

Sacrifice was, of course, known in all ancient cultures. And the sacrifices of Israel bear many resemblances in form and terminology to those of its neighbors. However, one must distinguish between form and meaning. The basic purpose of sacrifice in Israel was different from that in Mesopotamia or Canaan. In Mesopotamia and Canaan the sacrifice was usually a meal offered to a god to provide nourishment and strength. Since the god was dependent upon humans, sacrifice was a good way to influence the god to perform beneficial acts for the offerer. In Israel there was no concept, except perhaps in the popular mind, that God needed to be fed. It is the constant assertion that God is not dependent upon humans, and that God was active before Israel ever sacrificed. (Notice Psalm 50:12-13.) So the theologians of Israel did not usually condemn the form of sacrifice, unless it involved human sacrifice (2 Kings 16:3) or was accompanied by sacred prostitution (Amos 2:7). The disapproval came when Israel sacrificed to other gods or with a false idea of Yahweh's needs.

It has often been stated that sacrifice, in biblical thought, is an external way of expressing what transpires in the relationship between God and humanity. There is one relationship, but different facets of it. Thus there are different kinds of sacrifices or offerings. Each of them stresses some aspect of the relation, although not without inclusion of one or more of the other aspects. Some have asked why God utilized sacrifice at all. It was bloody and cruel. There is no complete answer, although it can perhaps be explained as due partly to the stage of the history of humankind. Sacrifice was the people's way of relating to the gods; it was a natural form of worship. In the development of biblical humanity, God took humans where they were and led them beyond sacrifice. Yet sacrifice had provided a needed reminder that relationship with God is a life-or-death matter. There were two dominant ideas in sacrifice.

First, sacrifice was concerned with *forgiveness of sins.* When people had broken the covenant by disobedience to its terms, they came with offerings designed to express their repentance and desire for restoration. There were two such offerings, although the difference between them is not clear. One was the "sin offering" (Leviticus 4:1–5:13; 6:24-30; Numbers 15:22-29). The word "sin" means "a failure to reach a goal or target," and so this offering emphasized that the offerer had come short of the kind of life intended under the covenant with God. The other offering for forgiveness of sin was the "guilt offering" (Leviticus 5:14–6:7; 7:1-10; Numbers 5:5-8). The distinction between this and the sin offering is not certain, but there is indication in the word "guilt" that means "to incur a penalty or debt" and therefore stresses the idea of making reparation for wrongdoing. Perhaps along with the idea of forgiveness, this offering included the emphasis that sinful action withholds things from God and people. For example, the procedure in case of theft was for the guilty party to make restitution of that which had been stolen, plus one fifth of its value (Leviticus 6:1-7).

Second, sacrifice was concerned with *fellowship with God.* Worship of God consists not only in restoring the covenant broken by humanity's disobedience, but also in enjoying the benefits of that relationship that has been restored. Three offerings stressed different aspects of this. The first was the "burnt offering" (Leviticus 1:1-17; 6:8-13). This term is a translation of a word meaning "that which goes up," a reference to the smoke that ascended to God when the sacrifice was burned. The ritual prescribed that the whole animal be consumed by fire. This sacrifice is also called the "whole burnt offering" (Deuteronomy 33:10) or "holocaust." The meaning is partly involved in the total burning and also in the fact that the particular sacrifice was graded according to the wealth of the offerer, so that everyone could afford a sacrifice. This suggests that the purpose of the burnt offering was to provide a means for each person to express giving something irrevocably to God. Forgiveness of sins was present (Leviticus 1:4), but the dominant idea was the giving of a gift to the sovereign Lord of all of life. Everything is God's, but the burnt offering was a person's way of recognizing this. Thus, the pouring out of blood and the subsequent forgiveness of sins were part of the ritual of the burnt offering.

The gift idea is carried forward in the second offering dealing with fellowship, namely, the "cereal (literally, 'gift') offering" (Leviticus 2:1-16; 6:14-23; Numbers 15:1-16). This usually was offered along with the "burnt offering," consisted primarily of cereal or grain in various forms, and was accompanied by wine (Numbers 15:5). The offerer brought the material to the priest, who burned a small portion as a "memorial" (Leviticus 2:2) and then kept the rest for the support of the priesthood. The distinction in meaning between the "cereal" and "burnt" offerings is not certain. The fact that the cereal offering involved the staples of Israelite diet—grain, oil, wine—may suggest that it was intended to stress one's recognition that God was Lord of all the fields. The burning of the memorial portion would indicate that although God was sovereign over the fields, people still had to live from their produce. The burnt offering, in supplement, would emphasize that God was Lord of all of life. Its complete burning would stress that the offerer recognized this; yet life could go on because of the grace of God.

The third offering that stressed fellowship with God was the "peace offering" (Leviticus 3:1-17; 7:11-38). Here the idea of fellowship was particularly evident, for central to the ritual was a meal shared by the Lord, by the priests, and by the offerer, and some friends. The fat and the blood were given to the Lord, the breast and right leg to the priest, and the remainder was for the worshiper and the friends. There was no idea here, as in some primitive cultures, of sharing physically in the life of God by eating a sacred victim. Rather the point was that the worshipers had communion with God by sharing a meal. Malachi 1:7 calls it "the LORD's table." The point of this communion is expressed by the words "peace offering." "Peace" in Hebrew is not simply the cessation of hostilities, but suggests well-being in all of life. The offering was a means of fellowship with God in joyful gratitude for the blessings of life. And because life is varied, there were three kinds of peace offerings: thank offering (Leviticus 7:12-15; 22:29-30), votive offering, and freewill offering (Leviticus 7:16-17; 22:18-23). The distinction between these is not absolutely clear. Probably the first dealt with thanks for a specific benefit, the second with fulfilling a vow made if something were to be granted to the offerer, and the third with general devotion and gratefulness to God. (Other offerings stressed fellowship—firstfruits [Deuteronomy 26:1ff.] and tithes [Numbers 18:21–32; Deuteronomy 14:22-29].)

(b) *Festivals.* Closely associated with sacrificial worship were the principal festivals of Israel. Every nation finds that its unity is strengthened by the remembrance of basic events in its formation and continuing life. These tend to provide opportunities for reaffirmation of loyalty and for the development of determination for future accomplishment. In Israel there were incorporated through the years various festivals that stressed the distinctive elements of history and faith. It is difficult, however, to determine what elements in the festivals were original, for most festivals, religious or not, tend to add practices or customs as the years progress. Christmas and Easter are good examples of this in Christianity. The most detailed list of such festivals is found in Leviticus 23. This reflects the practice in postexilic days (late sixth century B.C. and following), since it is part of the Priestly Code. (Notice also Numbers 28–29.) But we also read descriptions in Exodus 23:14-17 and 34:18-26, which come from the period of the Judges, that is, the twelfth to eleventh centuries B.C. And there is a third calendar of festivals or feasts in Deuteronomy 16, which dates from the seventh century B.C. Another feast, Purim, was added sometime in the second century B.C. It is described in the Book of Esther. Thus we can notice to a degree the development in Israelite practice.

Israel was a religious community, and so it is not surprising that its whole life revolved around the tabernacle or temple. There were daily, weekly, and monthly services, as well as the great annual feasts. Three of these festivals call for special comment.

The *sabbath* (Exodus 20:8-11; 23:12; 31:12-17; 34:21; Leviticus 23:3; Numbers 28:9-10; Deuteronomy 5:12-14) was a time every seventh day when the daily offering was doubled in quantity. But it involved more than this. It was a day of cessation of labor, as the word "sabbath" is linked with the meaning "to rest." Its uniqueness in Israelite practice did not lie in a time set apart for rest. Virtually every culture keeps such a day. Its significance lay in the reason time was set apart; it was "a sabbath to the LORD" (Leviticus 23:3). It was one of the signs of the covenant relationship between the Lord and Israel, and its institution is found in both accounts of the Ten Commandments (Exodus 20:8-11; Deuteronomy 5:12-14). These were the charter laws of that covenant established at Mount Sinai. The observance of the sabbath was meant to be a time when Israelites would rest and remember. It showed, on the one hand, God's loving concern for all people; even the slave was exempted from work. But it also indicated, on the other hand, Israel's need to remember the source of its life. Exodus 20:11 says that the sabbath is to remember God's work as creator, while Deuteronomy 5:15 links the remembrance with God's work as redeemer from Egypt. After the destruction of the temple in 586 B.C., the sabbath came gradually to increase in importance. With no temple or sacrifice remaining, observance of the sabbath became a sign of one's allegiance to the covenant. The rules became more strict, so that by New Testament times the joy of sabbath remembrance (Isaiah 58:13) became lost in negative piety.

The *Passover* and *Unleavened Bread* (Leviticus 23:5-14) were originally two separate feasts but became two phases of one festival. The earliest texts speak of them separately (Exodus 23:15; 34:18, 25). The first mention of them together is in Ezekiel 45:21, so it was probably not before the seventh or sixth centuries B.C. that they were combined. With these two festivals we see a practice that was common in the Old Testament period—the adapting of a common custom to the worship of Yahweh. Passover, on the one hand, was apparently originally a springtime rite practiced by seminomadic shepherds in very ancient times. At full moon in the first month of the year a young lamb was sacrificed to obtain the divine blessing on the flocks. Blood was smeared on the tent poles to drive away evil spirits. And the rest of the details for the ritual given in Exodus 12:1-20 also suggest this desert origin—no priest or altar, the normal unleavened bread of nomads, the desert plants ("bitter herbs"), and the clothing. The feast of Unleavened Bread, on the other hand, was originally a springtime celebration practiced by the Canaanites as an agricultural festival after the crops had been gathered. It was a time of dedication of the firstfruits of the harvest to the gods; thus it marked the beginning of the barley harvest. The ritual for this is spelled out in Leviticus 23:9-14. Israel, however, made both of these festivals uniquely its own by relating them to the historical event of the Exodus. "One springtime there had been a startling intervention of God: he had brought Israel out of Egypt, and this divine intervention marked the beginning of Israel's history as a people, as God's Chosen People: this period of liberation reached its consummation when they settled in the Promised Land. The feasts of the Passover and of Unleavened Bread commemorated this event. . . ."[1] Thus Israel celebrated these combined festivals as a time of rejoicing in the harvest, and as a time for thanksgiving to God whose grace had made the harvest in Palestine possible.

The *Day of Atonement* (Leviticus 23:26-32) is not mentioned in any part of the Old Testament before the sixth century B.C. It may be that, because it was a day with special emphasis on forgiveness of sins for the nation and the priesthood, it first arose during the exile when the weight of corporate guilt was felt so strongly by the people. It is clear that the dominant note of the Day of Atonement was forgiveness. The actual ritual is described in Leviticus 16 where we read of two basic actions. There was *first* the ritual by which the sins of the priesthood, the people, and the tabernacle/temple were forgiven. The great use of blood in this rite stressed the obtaining of life by the giving of life. But there was a *second* symbolism. This involved two goats, one of which was offered as a sin offering "for the LORD" while the other was led off into the desert "for Azazel." The idea of forgiveness for sin is clear in the ritual of the first goat, but what about the goat for Azazel? It is probable that this was the name of a desert demon (the name occurs only here in Leviticus 16), since the desert was considered by the Israelites to be a dwelling for devils (Isaiah 13:21; 34:8-17). Since the ritual involved the transference of the people's sins to this goat (Leviticus 16:21-22), it probably symbolized the removal of sins away from the people. So forgiveness and removal were the two great ideas of the Day of Atonement.

(3) *The preparations for departure* (Numbers 1:1–10:10). The great section dealing with the events at Mount Sinai concludes with a description of the arrangements for the departure into the wilderness toward Canaan. It contains a catalog of the number and arrangement of the various tribes (1:1–2:34), a list of the number and special duties of the Levites (3:1–4:49), a collection of laws for special situations (5:1–6:21), a priestly blessing (6:22-27), arrangements for tabernacle worship (7:1–8:26), plans for Passover celebration (9:1-14), and instructions for the departure (9:15–10:10).

*3. **Wandering in the Wilderness (Numbers 10:11–36:13).*** After their relatively brief stay at Mount Sinai, the Israelites departed for Canaan. Although in geographical distance Canaan was not particularly far, Israel was not able to enter it for a generation. Internal dissension and fear caused the people to wander in the wilderness for about forty years before crossing the Jordan into the Promised Land. There are two broad movements in this wandering. The *first* was from Mount Sinai to an oasis called Kadesh-barnea in the Negeb (10:11–20:1). There Israel camped for about thirty-five years, during which time they attempted to attack the land of Canaan from the south and were repulsed (13:1–14:45). The *second* movement was from Kadesh to Trans-Jordan (20:2–36:13). The book ends with Israel camped on the eastern side of the Jordan river, ready to strike into Palestine. There probably was originally an account of the military conquest of Palestine to complete the Priestly story of promise and fulfillment. But this has now been replaced by the Book of Joshua.

One conspicuous theme of the wilderness wandering is "complaint." It is a theme that has appeared earlier. After the escape from Egypt, the people began to panic in face of the precarious existence in the desert (Exodus 16–18). They grumbled about the need for water (Exodus 15:22-27; 17:1-7), for food (Exodus 16:1-36), and for protection (Exodus 17:8-16). When the people were stopped at Mount Sinai, they complained about the long delay of Moses in returning from the mountain (Exodus 32:1-35). In similar fashion the people of Israel complained after their departure from Mount Sinai. Again they faced the problems of water (Numbers 20:2-13), of food (11:1-35), and of protection (13:1–14:45). But a new problem arose—leadership. Various challenges were made against the placing of Moses and Aaron at the head of the people (12:1-16; 16:1–17:13). Each challenge was thrown aside with rather startling results.

But there is another dominant theme in the wandering accounts—"the power of the LORD." And it is around these two ideas of "complaint" and "divine power" that the wilderness wandering stories are to be read. On the one hand, we read of a series of internal and external threats to the existence of the Chosen People. The Abrahamic promise seems about to be thwarted. But then, on the other hand, we read of a series of divine miracles and interventions that keep Israel alive and moving forward. God will not allow the divine promise to go unfulfilled. So the thirst is satisfied by water from the rock; the hunger is assuaged by manna and quails; and the threats to leadership are mollified by spectacular punishments. Yet complaint and lack of faith are not without their consequences. This lesson is brought to its clearest focus in the abortive attack on Canaan from the south (Numbers 13:1–14:45). Twelve scouts were sent by Moses to spy out the land of Canaan to see if an attack would be feasible. Two of the scouts, Joshua and Caleb, reported that the Israelites could take the land; but the rest thought the land too formidable. Faced with this news, the people began to complain and to talk about choosing a leader to take them back to Egypt. They refused to put any faith in the presence of the Lord. Even after the series of great miracles they had experienced, the people were not really certain that Yahweh was capable of seeing them through to the Promised Land. The result was that the rebellious and faithless people were condemned to spend the rest of their lives in the wilderness. The promise would not be destroyed, but it could be delayed (14:20-38).

This double theme of "complaint" and "divine power" is picked up throughout the rest of the Old Testament. Sometimes the first is stressed; Psalm 106:13-33 describes the rebelliousness of the people. But at other times the second theme is emphasized. This thought lies behind Joshua's words regarding the great deeds of God (Joshua 24:8-10). And Jeremiah even speaks of a third aspect when he describes the period of wandering as one in which the people were devoted to the Lord (Jeremiah 2:2). This can only be understood as the prophet's overstated attempt to show that Israel's leadership was once loyal to the Lord.

So the theological point of the wilderness wandering is this: Lack of faith in God brings disaster and delay in the good life. Only when one shows trust in God by obedience to God's will can there be individual hope for the future.

- What were the "Priestly" historians trying to communicate? How does the life of Jacob specifically illustrate this? What are primary and secondary lessons in his life?
- What emphases in the creation stories speak to our present scientific and technological world? Consider the view of God, of humankind, and of the natural world.
- How do the Old Testament laws help us to make ethical decisions? Remember the distinction between the general ideas of the Decalogue and the specific applications in the Covenant Code. Do we try to apply the form or the intent?
- What were various aspects of the relation with God that sacrificial worship expressed? How does present church life provide means for the expression of similar concepts?

Additional Resources

Brueggemann, Walter. *Genesis.* Atlanta: John Knox Press, 1982.

Childs, Brevard S. *The Book of Exodus: A Critical, Theological Commentary.* Philadelphia: Westminster Press, 1974.

Clines, David J. A. *The Theme of the Pentateuch.* Journal for the Study of the Old Testament Supplement Series: No. 10. Sheffield: Journal for the Study of the Old Testament Press, 1978.

Ellis, Peter F. *The Yahwist: The Bible's First Theologian.* Notre Dame, Ind.: Fides, 1968.

Friedman, Richard E. *Who Wrote the Bible?* New York: Harper & Row, 1989.

Noth, Martin. *Leviticus: A Commentary.* Philadelphia: Westminster Press, 1977.

Noth, Martin. *Numbers: A Commentary.* Translated by James D. Martin. Philadelphia: Westminster Press, 1968.

Porter, J. R. *Leviticus.* Cambridge: Cambridge University Press, 1976.

Thielicke, Helmut. *How the World Began.* Philadelphia: Fortress Press, 1961.

Westermann, Claus. *Genesis.* Grand Rapids: William B. Eerdmans, 1987.

Vawter, Bruce. *On Genesis: A New Reading.* Garden City, N.Y.: Doubleday, 1977.

2

THE DEUTERONOMIC HISTORY

Deuteronomy–Kings

The book of Deuteronomy provides the introduction and grand plan for another historical section, namely, the Deuteronomic History. It covers the material in Joshua, Judges, First and Second Samuel, and First and Second Kings, and deals with the whole history of Israel in the land of Palestine from its entrance in the thirteenth century B.C. to its exit in the sixth century B.C. At some unknown time and place after the destruction of Jerusalem by the Babylonians in 587 B.C., a group of survivors began to reflect on the recent events. The temple had been destroyed, the nation had been ravaged, and many of the people had been exiled. Why? Who had failed? What had brought about the destructive events? What did the future hold? Apparently they remembered the words of the prophets whose warnings and explanations had been rejected for centuries. The prophets had been right! The nation had met the fate that the prophets saw as inevitable in light of the personal and national conduct of the people. So from this prophetic perspective the Deuteronomic History was written.

This group of Israelites gathered together many of the old traditions, edited and revised them, and put together a comprehensive history from the last days of Moses, as the people stood poised to enter the land, to the last days of the nation, as the people were dragged off to exile from the land. Their concern, therefore, was with Israel and the land of Palestine. ". . . The burden of their writing is the theology of the land, the terms on which it is to be occupied, and the special temptations and blessings it offers."[2] They sought to present to their generation the lessons of history they had learned, and thus to give them some hope for a meaningful future. Their point was simple: History is determined by obedience or disobedience to the Lord. Only wholehearted obedience to the Lord, illustrated in everyday morality and exclusive worship centered at Jerusalem, could give blessing and national permanence. This philosophy is spelled out in the speeches in 1 Samuel 12 and 1 Kings 8:31-53. Hence, the books from Joshua through Second Kings are called the "Former Prophets." These books proclaim a theological message in the midst of their historical narration.

The book of Deuteronomy provides the key to the history of Israel. The divine standards laid down on its pages, which Israel solemnly swore to obey (Deuteronomy 27:15-26), give the norm by which the events in the land of Palestine are to be judged. This norm is epitomized in Deuteronomy 30:15-20. Then, in light of this norm, the Book of Joshua stresses the theme of blessing; Israel was successful in the land because of obedience. But Judges through Kings emphasize the theme of judgment; Israel suffered and ultimately lost the land because of disobedience. The blessings of the promise were taken away (Deuteronomy 30:19-20) for failure to meet the terms of the promise—obedience. The particular example used to illustrate this was the relationship of the kings of Israel and Judah to idol worship. All the kings of Israel, write the historians, failed to keep the worship pure, and only two in Judah (Hezekiah and Josiah) gained approval. Sometimes moralizing is direct (1 Kings 16:8-14, 18-19, 25-26), sometimes indirect (2 Samuel 9–20; 1 Kings 1–2). Samuel is less moralizing than the rest of the books because David is the hero in three-fourths of the book, and he was an ideal king by the historians' standards.

Although the Priestly History (Genesis–Numbers) and the Deuteronomic History (Deuteronomy–Kings) provide two large historical blocks, the final formation of the Old Testament joined Deuteronomy to the first four books to form what is called the "Pentateuch." It is to this collection of five books that the New Testament writers refer when they speak of the "Law" (Matthew 7:12). The reason the books were grouped in this fashion is not clear, although it may have been that Deuteronomy closes with the death of Moses. Thus Genesis through Deuteronomy forms a collection around the person of Moses.

THE DEUTERONOMIC PLAN

The book of Deuteronomy is shaped in the form of a series of speeches by Moses to the Israelites as they encamped east of the Jordan River (Deuteronomy 1:1-5). His purpose was to restate the Law, to explain its implications for the new life facing the people in Palestine, and to warn the people that their obedience or disobedience would determine the fate of the society they would soon be establishing. The name "Deuteronomy" means "second law" and comes from the Septuagint, a Greek version of the Bible from the third and second centuries B.C. But this title is misleading, for the book does not claim to be a second law, but rather a restatement of the first law. The problem arose because the Septuagint mistranslated a phrase in Deuteronomy 17:18 that reads: ". . . [the king] shall write for himself in a book a copy of this law." The Septuagint translated the last phrase as "this second law."

The book of Deuteronomy played a major role in the spiritual life of Judah. In 621 B.C., King Josiah was in the midst of seeking to reform the nation of its idol worship. While making repairs on the temple, workers discovered "the book of the law" in some rubbish that was to be thrown out (2 Kings 22:3-9). This book was shown to Josiah and became the major basis of his reforms. Most scholars assume that this "book of the law" was, for the most part, the book of Deuteronomy, since the goals of the reform mentioned in 2 Kings 22–23 find many parallels with Deuteronomy. Obviously the book originated sometime earlier, but where and by whom are uncertain.

The Deuteronomic plan, which provides the key to the whole history of Israel from Joshua through Second Kings, has three facets. *First,* it commands that all foreign gods must be exterminated from Israel because there is only one god—Yahweh (Deuteronomy 6:4-5; 1 Samuel 12). *Second,* there must be only one sanctuary where Yahweh is worshiped (Deuteronomy 12). *Third,* worship of Yahweh must be verified by everyday justice and morality (Deuteronomy 5–26). This was the constitution of the people of God. If they wished to remain in the land of Palestine, if they wished to build a stable society, they had to remain loyal to these terms (Deuteronomy 8). The history in Joshua through Second Kings shows us what happened to the people in the light of this choice.

THE CONQUEST OF PALESTINE (JOSHUA)

The Book of Joshua presents the story of the conquest of Palestine under the leadership of Joshua (1–12), tells how the land was divided among the twelve tribes (13–22), and concludes with two miscellaneous chapters dealing with Joshua's last address to the people (23) and a great covenant renewal service at the town of Shechem in central Palestine (24). This service was necessary in order for the generation which had not been at Mount Sinai to express its own faith in the Lord and its commitment to the covenant relationship.

The Book of Joshua helps us to see that the biblical historians were also theologians. What the writers have presented is a story of actual events, to be sure, but the events have been depicted so as to emphasize the involvement of the Lord. The writers have tried to show that the conquest was the fulfillment of the old promises to Abraham, Isaac, and Jacob. They have spent so much time on the details of the allocation of the land to the tribes because these were not mere lists but were thrilling accounts of God's faithfulness and goodness and power. So the account of the distribution of land concludes with the words: "Thus the LORD gave to Israel all the land which he swore to give to their fathers; and having taken possession of it, they settled there" (Joshua 21:43; compare to 21:45). The promises are not given automatically, but they presuppose that people must work and fulfill the conditions by which the promise can become a reality.

The theological purpose of showing God's involvement in Israel's history helps us to understand another fact about the book. According to the authors, the conquest of Palestine was rapid, complete, and accomplished by all the tribes. Yet here and there one reads a comment that the conquest was not so sweeping and complete. The Canaanites still remained in control of various areas, and sometimes only later were subdued (Joshua 13:2-6; 15:63; 16:10; 17:11-13; 23:7-13). Furthermore, although Joshua 10:36-39 states that "all Israel" captured Hebron and Debir, Judges 1:9-15 claims that the tribe of Judah took these places. All these bits of evidence are in line with the story in Judges 2 that the conquest was a slow process, with many failures and loss of territory. What does all this mean? It means simply that we must read the Book of Joshua as a theological document. It means that Israel accomplished the conquest of the land because of loyalty to the Lord who blessed Israel's endeavors. This is the Deuteronomic theology of history—success comes when people are faithful to God. So the authors, although cognizant of the facts of a slow conquest (it was not completed until 300 years later during the days of David), ignored many of the details in order to teach their lesson that obedience and loyalty bring blessing. They heightened or stressed the miraculous character of the conquest so that the events are not always depicted exactly as they happened. The capture of Jericho through the collapse of its walls is a witness to God's activity in the conquest, even though we cannot be sure about all the details. Joshua 10:12-14 is another example of God's involvement. What in context (10:6-11) was a hailstorm, described poetically as the "standing still" (literally, "ceasing, becoming silent") of the sun and moon, becomes in the final comment of the editor a miracle of cosmological extent—the sun and moon actually stopped in the heavens (10:13-14)! We miss the writers' meaning, therefore, when we attempt to make a one-for-one relationship between success and righteousness. They knew this was not true, but sought by overstatement to teach a general lesson about joy and obedience to the Lord.

The disparity between Joshua and Judges concerning the conquest of Palestine, however, should not cause us to forget that we are still reading history. Many of the details have been obscured, but nevertheless the basic events took place. Archaeological work has given us a great deal of evidence that there was a widespread onslaught into Palestine between 1250 and 1200 B.C. Many of the cities said to have been taken by the Israelites at this time, such as Eglon, Debir, and Lachish, show signs of severe destruction. So although archaeology does not prove that Israel conquered the land, it nevertheless gives us evidence that is, in general, consistent with the biblical record.

The theological purpose, although helping us to understand some aspects of the account of Israel's history in the Book of Joshua, nevertheless raises a problem. If the authors are attempting to show the involvement of the Lord in the history of Israel, then these accounts appear to tell us that God was the cause of the slaughter of thousands of Canaanites, many of them women and children. We are told that the Lord commanded them to enter into the land of Palestine (Joshua 1:2) and gave them victory (Joshua 10:14). God is depicted, therefore, both as a God of faithfulness and as a God of war (see Exodus 15:3; 23:23-33). How are we to understand this? It will help us if we can always remember as we read the Old Testament that although it is the Word of God, not everything it records is the will of God. One of the great values of the Old Testament is that it presents to us a picture of human beings, not fairy-tale creatures. The Israelites, though related to God, shared in many of the prejudices, social mores, and political ideas of their neighbors. God did not choose Israel in a moral vacuum, nor take them out of the morality of their times. God chose real, imperfect men and women who were living in a certain culture and sought to make them the agents of divine purposes. God does the same with people today. Relationship with God does not mean perfection, nor the removal of false ideas. It means the beginning of a process of development towards that about which we may know nothing at the time. Good Christian people endorsed slavery for centuries, believing it to be the will of God. So Israel shared in the ideas of its day about warfare. They believed in the "holy war," as did all of their neighbors. It was not their intent, as with some peoples, to spread their faith by force of arms, yet they believed that God fought for them and received the fruits of victory (Joshua 6:17-24). But why would God fight and conquer? The answer was clear: because of the wickedness of the people and because of God's determination to fulfill the promises (Deuteronomy 9:1-5). But at this point the reading of the Old Testament is difficult. Somehow one has to keep in balance the sovereignty of God and the freedom of humanity. On the one hand, the Old Testament persistently affirms that God is involved in the course of history, and yet, on the other hand, it is also clear that humans affect that history; humans are free to do things contrary to the will of God and even to claim God's approval of evil or incorrect actions (see Jeremiah 27–28; particularly 28:11-15). Thus we have to make an important distinction between the basic purposes of God and the way those purposes are carried out. What is certain is that wickedness is punished and that God's promises are fulfilled. This is foundational to the biblical view of God's sovereignty. But what is not so certain is that God punishes wickedness or fulfills goals by sending a slaughtering army. When the Israelites claimed this, it may well have been out of their own cultural blindness to the character of God. It was easy enough to claim God's will and be wrong. Job's friends had to be rebuked for this (Job 42:7). And indeed later in the Old Testament the philosophy of the "holy war" was repudiated (Ezekiel 18:23). So the Old Testament is a story of God working with people and nations and seeking to lead them to something higher and finer. In the meantime, as is true with us as well, human prejudices and hates and blindnesses will inevitably be present. We may be clear about God's purposes, but we may also incorrectly assume that we know how those purposes are being carried out. Israel believed God wanted them to enter the land of Canaan, and this was certainly true. But Israel too quickly assumed that God wanted a holy war against Canaan's inhabitants.

THE PERIOD OF THE JUDGES (JUDGES)

The conquest of Palestine did not mean the establishment of a state. This was not to come until the time of David. Between Joshua and David there was a unique period in Israel's existence, covering most of the twelfth and eleventh centuries B.C., when the seminomadic people sought to adjust to more settled life. It was a wild, barbarous time, when "there was no king in Israel; every man did what was right in his own eyes" (Judges 21:25). The details are given in four sections of the Book of Judges. The book opens with a piecemeal account of the conquest of Palestine (1:1–2:5), somewhat different in tenor from the Book of Joshua. As we saw in the last section, here we read not of a sweeping, complete conquest, but of a drawn-out, incomplete victory. Some tribes were able to capture the areas into which they came, but others could only infiltrate and settle down side by side with the native Canaanites. Furthermore, there were almost continuous, though intermittent, battles for even those able to gain some military foothold. This account is probably close to what actually happened; conquest was a protracted affair. This description provides a preface or background to the main story of the book and explains the reason for the unsettled times reflected in that story. They "could not drive out the inhabitants of the plain, because they had chariots of iron" (Judges 1:19).

The second section of the book (Judges 2:6–3:6) is actually the introduction to the period of the judges. As 2:6 shows clearly, it is the sequel to the account in Joshua 24, for it tells what happened "when Joshua dismissed the people." (Compare Judges 2:6 with Joshua 24:28.) This indicates that Judges 1:1–2:5 as well as Joshua 24:29-33 were additional materials added after the Deuteronomic History was broken up into separate books. The purpose of this introductory section is theological; it seeks to give us a lesson from history about the results of Israel's loyalty or lack of loyalty to God. The author's point is this: Whenever the Israelites forgot the Lord and turned to idol worship, they were allowed to fall into the hands of an enemy who oppressed them for some years. But when Israel repented and prayed to the Lord, God raised up for them a deliverer or "judge," who then led them and kept them faithful. But inevitably after the death of the deliverer the people once again turned to idols, and just as certainly the cycle of apostasy, oppression, repentance, and deliverance was repeated. To those in later times who read this story, the lesson was clear: Israel's security in the face of its enemies lay in loyalty to the covenantal relationship with the Lord. This theme is not simply theological speculation, but a sound view of life based on solid experience. Idol worship or Baalism was disruptive to social unity. Such religion made few personal demands apart from sacrifice and left the worshipers free to do what they wished. Consequently, tribal jealousies and the desire for personal aggrandizement tended to weaken the solidarity of the scattered groups of Israelites. All idols, since they are the creation of humans, tend to do this. But the worship of the Lord was a unifying force since it bound the tribes together in common commitment and loyalty outside themselves.

The third section (Judges 3:7–16:31) is the main body of the book, giving us the accounts of the various deliverers or judges. Here we are reading hero stories, not sober history. There is a great deal of stylization. The length of each judge's rule is either twenty, forty, or eighty years, and their reigns are depicted generally as following one another and as having been exercised over all the tribes. In point of fact, many of them probably ruled at the same time over different areas, and so the period of the judges may have been shorter than the numbers suggest. Again this reminds us of the rich variety of the biblical literature. These stories are exuberant accounts of great heroes, and historical details are subordinated to the storyteller's art or are expanded and exaggerated, as in the life of Samson, to depict superhuman figures.

One meets in this section two kinds of "judges," a term which means "adjudicator," "ruler," "helper," and thus one who both administers and secures justice in the fullest sense. The first kind of judge, and the most prominent, was the charismatic hero. These were the military leaders whom God raised up to lead a resistance movement against an oppressive enemy. After having delivered the tribe or tribes, these judges continued to exercise a measure of authority over the people. Their military prowess had demonstrated their special relationship with God. As was noticed, their authority apparently was not accepted over all the tribes, but only over those they had delivered from an enemy. There are eight of these in the book—Othniel, Ehud, Shamgar, Deborah, Gideon, Abimelech, Jephthah, and Samson.

The second kind of judge was the governmental official. These were the magistrates whose function was to interpret the law, to adjudicate matters of controversy between tribes and clans, and to handle other governmental affairs. They were not associated with a particular tribe and apparently were situated in different cities or regions. The information on these leaders is sparse; perhaps they were elected officials (see Judges 10:1-5; 12:7-15). There are seven mentioned in the book: Gideon, Tola, Jair, Jephthah, Ibzan, Elon, and Abdon. Two of these, Gideon and Jephthah, were also charismatic heroes.

The cultural and religious situation during the period of the judges is not absolutely clear. It is certain, however, that there was no unified political state. The tribes remained relatively independent of each other; some became farmers and city dwellers, while others continued as seminomads. Each tribe had to struggle to conquer and maintain its own assigned territory. Yet they were not without their unity based upon their common faith and commitment to the covenant established at Mount Sinai. So in times of military crisis a judge would arise to call neighboring tribes to help a given tribe fight for the Lord (Judges 5:23). Some scholars have suggested that this unity is best described in terms of an "amphictyony." This is a Greek word denoting an association of tribes or groups united around a central shrine to which representatives from each tribe would gather periodically to renew allegiance to the covenant and to iron out matters of controversy. Shiloh, a town in centrally located Ephraim, was perhaps such a shrine (Judges 18:31; 1 Samuel 1–3).

The book closes with two supplementary accounts of events during the days of the judges (17–18 and 19–21). They do not deal directly with any of the charismatic heroes or governmental officials, but are incidents illustrating the fact that in those days "every man did what was right in his own eyes" (17:6; 21:25).

THE MONARCHY (1 SAMUEL 1–1 KINGS 11)

The tribes were able to exist for about two hundred years in Canaan in their independent, scattered condition. But recurrent idolatry and tribal jealousies tended to weaken the unity they had under their common faith, and increasing pressure by other inhabitants of Canaan, the Philistines, finally brought about their subjugation (1 Samuel 4). The ark was captured, Philistine garrisons were stationed at key places, and all metal industry was forbidden lest the Israelites arm themselves for revolt (1 Samuel 13:19-22). The good old days of independence were gone. So the elders of Israel recognized that a new form of political organization was necessary if the people were to survive. They requested a king to unify them and to lead them to freedom from the Philistines (1 Samuel 8:5-6). The story of these events, and of the monarchy that resulted, is presented in 1 Samuel 1–1 Kings 11. Most of the action revolves around the lives and interrelations of four figures—Samuel, Saul, David, Solomon. It is not, however, to be forgotten that this section is part of the Former Prophets, so one will notice two elements interlacing throughout. One of these is that this section is the history of the monarchy, a period covering from 1020 (rise of Saul) to 922 B.C. (death of Solomon). For this history many kinds of material have been used, including poems or prayers (1 Samuel 2:1-10; 2 Samuel 1:19-27), songs (2 Samuel 22:1-51; 23:1-7), and biography (1 Samuel 1–3), and narratives (1 Samuel 4–6; 2 Samuel 9–20; 1 Kings 1–2). But this section also contains the history of the prophets covering the same period. There are only three prophets mentioned specifically—Samuel (1 Samuel 1–15), Nathan, and Gad (2 Samuel 7, 12, 24)—but actually prophetic influence is felt all the way through in the way the history has been written. This is Deuteronomic History, and thus the prophetic, and perhaps priestly, viewpoint constantly seeks to show the theological lessons to be gained from the events of the monarchy.

1. Samuel. The first section (1 Samuel 1–7) concerns the rise of Samuel to authority and influence. Samuel provided a basic link in the transition between the days of the judges and the monarchy, for he fulfilled two offices that brought about the change. *First,* he was a judge who was probably both a charismatic hero and a governmental official, as Gideon and Jephthah had been. He spent his early years at Shiloh under the tutelage of the old priest Eli, and during this time the pressure of the Philistines was increasing. Finally, after the Philistines destroyed Shiloh and captured the ark (1 Samuel 4), Samuel rallied the tribes and drove the Philistines from the territory (1 Samuel 7:3-14). Having demonstrated his authority, he continued the rest of his life to function as an administrator and adjudicator (1 Samuel 7:15-17). But, *second,* Samuel also became the founder of the prophetic movement. As a boy at Shiloh he had received the call of the Lord to be the divine spokesperson (1 Samuel 3:1–4:1). And thereafter Samuel proclaimed the word of the Lord, announcing judgment (1 Samuel 3:10–4:1; 15:1 and the following verses), instructing as to the way of the Lord (1 Samuel 10:25), and passionately calling the people to repentance and obedience to the covenant (1 Samuel 12:1-25). As a man both acquainted with the struggles of survival under the leadership of judges and well-known as a spokesman for the Lord, Samuel understandably became the one to whom the people turned for the selection of a king.

2. Saul. The second section (1 Samuel 8–2 Samuel 1) deals with the elevation of Saul to the kingship and with the problems that developed out of this selection. Here was a real test of Samuel's character and of his ability to move with the times. The judge-prophet had grown old and had turned over his judicial duties to his two sons. But their ineffectiveness and corruptness, and the menace of the Philistines, caused the people to come to Samuel and demand a new form of government—kingship (1 Samuel 8:1-6). Samuel's response to this, and the eventual choice of Saul as king, are somewhat confused by the fact that the writers of the book have drawn on two different traditions of the events. One tradition depicts Samuel as bitterly opposed to the request, seeing it as a rejection of the Lord (1 Samuel 8:1-22; 10:17-27; 12:1-25). The other tradition describes the monarchy as a joyous gift from the Lord to save God's people from disaster (1 Samuel 9:1–10:16; 11:1-15). Here we see a good example of the historian's art and of the accuracy of Scripture. Apparently the change from the rule of the judges to the rule of a king was not without its controversy. A radical break with tradition such as this must have evoked opposition. Even Samuel himself must have had mixed feelings. So the author attempted to reflect the whole situation—kingship was God's gift at a crucial period in history, but kingship was not without its problems.

Saul's reign did not produce a true monarchy, for he was never really a king. He was more a charismatic judge in the old style, except that his rule embraced all the tribes. He came to power by a smashing victory over the Ammonites (1 Samuel 11) and continued throughout the rest of his life as a chieftain rallying the tribes against common foes. He had no real palace nor kingdom, but engaged in guerilla raids and battles from a sanctuary at Gibeah in the central highlands. Although he started off with brilliant military success and personal attractiveness, Saul never could establish a stable rule, for he was constantly at odds with those whom he needed. First, it was Samuel whom he alienated by his failure to accept the old judge's role as priest (1 Samuel 13:8-14) and prophet (1 Samuel 15). Then it was David whom he drove from his side because of his cancerous jealousy over the young warrior's popularity, so that in Saul's final battle against the Philistines he had to fight without the support of David and his troops (1 Samuel 16–31). And, of course, through it all Saul was fighting himself. Subject to moods of depression and self-doubt, he constantly wrestled with "an evil spirit from the LORD [that] tormented him" (1 Samuel 16:14). From these times of mental conflict David was often able to rouse him by playing the lyre. But in the end Saul's mind deteriorated, convinced that the Lord had passed him by, as Samuel had said (1 Samuel 13:13-14).

3. David. The third section (2 Samuel 2–1 Kings 2) describes the golden age of David's reign. Here for the first time a true monarchy was established. Actually David's rise to power began early in Saul's reign, and much of the account in 1 Samuel 16–31 is concerned to point this out. His skill as a musician, his military successes, his friendship with Saul's son Jonathan, and his marriage to Saul's daughter Michal all depict for us a capable and attractive person. So it is not surprising that after the death of Saul, David was chosen as king. However, here something needs to be noticed. David's choice as king over all the tribes was not automatic. At first only his own tribe of Judah anointed him as king (2 Samuel 2:1-4), and for seven years and six months his reign was therefore localized (2 Samuel 5:5). Apparently the old tribal jealousies erupted after the death of Saul, for Saul's son Ishbosheth initially became king over the other tribes (2 Samuel 2:8-10). It is interesting to note, by the way, that Saul's son is called "Eshbaal" in 1 Chronicles 8:33 and elsewhere. This was probably his actual name, for it became the practice in some texts for later scribes to eliminate the hated name "baal" and to substitute "bosheth" (shame). "Ish" and "Esh" are basically the same word.

For some time there was a struggle between David and Eshbaal (2 Samuel 3:1), but finally Eshbaal was assassinated (2 Samuel 4). In the face of the continued threat of the Philistines, the other tribes came to David at Hebron and offered him the kingship (2 Samuel 5). Their choice was natural, for as they themselves admitted, "In times past, when Saul was king over us, it was you that led and brought in Israel; and the LORD said to you, 'You shall be shepherd of my people Israel, and you shall be prince over Israel' " (2 Samuel 5:2). Yet it was always somewhat of an uneasy alliance and was only established on the basis of a covenant that implied the possibility of being dissolved (2 Samuel 5:3). This history provides an important background to understanding the later breakup of the monarchy into the kingdoms of Judah and Israel at the death of Solomon.

Although it began with struggle, David's reign over all Israel was a great success. His initial act as king was a shrewd one. Having conquered the Jebusite city of Jerusalem on the border between the northern and southern tribes, he established it as the political and religious center of the land. Now he was able to centralize his authority at a neutral site instead of at the more remote Judean city of Hebron in the south. And by bringing the ark from Kiriath-jearim to Jerusalem (2 Samuel 6), he was also able to unify religious loyalties at a place that did not always remind the northern tribes of his Judean heritage.

The rest of David's reign is a story of expansion and consolidation. He was able to extend the boundaries to include not only all of western Palestine, but also the kingdoms of Moab, Edom, and Ammon to the east, and Syria to the north. Furthermore he made an alliance with the Phoenicians and relegated the Philistines to a small territory on the western seacoast. For the first time in its history Palestine became a single kingdom, stable and secure.

David was not without his foibles, and the historian of his reign clearly admits these. David took an inexplicable dislike to his general Joab, a man who had saved him from military blunders on many occasions, and on his deathbed David ordered Joab killed (1 Kings 2:5-6). His adulterous affair with Bathsheba and his murder of her husband Uriah are well known (2 Samuel 11–13). Yet the historian can record that the Lord chose David because he was "a man after his own heart" (1 Samuel 13:14). And it was to David that the Lord said: "Your house and your kingdom shall be made sure for ever before me; your throne shall be established for ever" (2 Samuel 7:16). Here is something profound and important: David was a great man, blessed by God, not because he was perfect, but because he could always admit his faults and demonstrate a basic sincerity and desire to be a servant of God. This is emphasized in his response to Nathan the prophet. After Nathan had pointed an accusing finger at him for his affair with Bathsheba, David replied, "I have sinned against the LORD" (2 Samuel 12:13). In his repentance and acceptance of his punishment we see illustrated the basic concern for obedient relationship with God that lay at the heart of his greatness as a leader. But in the disruptive effects that his conduct had on his sons Absalom and Amnon (2 Samuel 13–18), we also have depicted for us the inexorable law of life that no sin is private.

4. Solomon. The last part (1 Kings 3–11) is an account of the reign of Solomon. This is a very selected description taken from what was once probably a much longer story called "the book of the acts of Solomon" (1 Kings 11:41). The account really begins in 1 Kings 1–2. As David became decrepit with old age, there arose a struggle for power among rival factions. On the one side was Adonijah, David's oldest son and the natural heir. He was supported by Joab the general and the priest Abiathar. On the other side was Solomon, the son of David and Bathsheba, supported by the prophet Nathan and the priest Zadok. David apparently desired Solomon as his successor, and on his deathbed gave Solomon a charge that is reflective of the whole Deuteronomic History: Obedience to the Lord is the way to success (1 Kings 2:1-12). At the death of David, the young Solomon quickly exerted his control. He had Adonijah and Joab killed, and banished Abiathar to his ancestral home. Thus "the kingdom was established in the hand of Solomon" (1 King 2:46*b*).

Solomon's reign is somewhat enigmatic; and the reason is perhaps epitomized in 1 Kings 3:3: "Solomon loved the LORD, walking in the statutes of David his father; only, he sacrificed and burnt incense at the high places." The point is that Solomon had two very strong sides to his character. On the one hand, he clearly recognized his own inadequacy to rule apart from the help of God. He stated this openly at the beginning of his reign (1 Kings 3:6-9). And this dependence upon God is given as the reason for his wisdom and consequent success (1 Kings 3:10-14). As one reads the account of Solomon's rule, there is no question that he exhibited great wisdom (1 Kings 3–4) and concern for God, the latter emphasized in the building of the temple (1 Kings 5–8). The result of all this, as the Deuteronomic historian saw it, was that the Lord blessed him with great political and economic success. Looked at from this point of view, the Solomonic kingdom was magnificent. He was able to extend the borders of Israel even farther than his father David had. He brought in a high level of culture. International trade was facilitated by his fleet of ships (1 Kings 9:26). Solomon became a patron of the arts of song and proverb (1 Kings 4:32; compare Psalms 72, 127; Proverbs 1:1). He engaged in great building projects, including not only the temple and the royal palace in Jerusalem, but also "store" and "chariot cities" (1 Kings 9:18-19; 10-26). Abundant evidence of warehouse cities has been unearthed by the archaeologists. The remains of a copper refinery have also been discovered in the area of the Jordan (see 1 Kings 7:46). And he sought to lessen any threat from foreign invasion by entering into a political marriage with the daughter of the Egyptian pharaoh (1 Kings 3:1; 7:8; 9:16).

On the other hand, Solomon sought a life independent of God. The tremendous international and internal achievements were an attempt at self-aggrandizement. Human life was cheap and could be easily sacrificed to foster the advancement of his rule. Perhaps one can see this from the beginning in his ruthless extermination of all rivals, although this was not uncommon procedure in the ancient world. But Solomon brought in a new kind of kingship. Saul's court, as we saw, was relatively simple with little governmental interference in the life of the people. David unified the tribes and established more of a centralized authority (see 2 Samuel 20:23-26). But Solomon brought in virtual despotism, with a court of servants and officials and a harem that separated him from the people as a whole. He began to look upon his subjects as slaves to fulfill his personal ambitions for glory. Immense tax burdens were imposed, forced labor was instituted, and the country was divided into twelve districts to supply food for the king and his household (1 Kings 4:7-19; 5:13-14; 9:15; 11:28).

Solomon's reign was ultimately tragic. He was a brilliant man who brought previously unknown grandeur to his country. He understood the need for loyalty to the Lord and stressed this in his moving prayer at the dedication of the temple (1 Kings 8, especially verses 56-61). But his great natural ability and knowledge increasingly became perverted by selfishness, greed, and inhumanity, so that finally his wisdom became overshadowed by stupid political and economic decisions. There is no question that a root cause was his large harem of foreign women. The Deuteronomic historian claims that their worship of other gods finally influenced Solomon (1 Kings 11:1-8). Solomon came to accept a pagan theology, namely, a view of God as a despot unconcerned about the lives of individuals, worshiped by gifts of food and supported by immoral cultic practices. He built a kingdom on a rotten foundation of oppression and indulgence, so that before his death, territories began to fall away (1 Kings 11:14-25), and after his death the kingdom divided into two. The historian is careful to point out why: "The LORD was angry with Solomon, because his heart had turned away from the LORD, the God of Israel. . . . Therefore the LORD said to Solomon . . . I will surely tear the kingdom from you and will give it to your servant" (1 Kings 11:9, 11).

THE DIVIDED KINGDOM (1 KINGS 12–2 KINGS 25)

The death of Solomon in 922 B.C. brought about not so much a struggle for power as an attempt by some to alleviate the oppressive policies of Solomon. The refusal by Solomon's successor and son, Rehoboam, to do this caused an irreparable split and division of the monarchy into two separate kingdoms. At the death of his father, Rehoboam went to Shechem to be anointed as king (1 Kings 12:1). Shechem was the chief city of the northern tribes (Joshua 24:1, 32), and Rehoboam needed to gain the allegiance of the northern tribes if the monarchy was to continue. As we saw earlier, Judah in the south and the other tribes in the north had established a covenant of alliance during the days of David. But it was not an unbreakable covenant and had to be renewed at the accession of each king. So it was that the tribes gathered at Shechem to decide the future of the monarchy. Under the leadership of Jeroboam, a former officer under Solomon, the northern tribes demanded a reduction in taxation and forced labor. Rehoboam rejected this condition, having been imbued with the despotic ideas of his father. So the northern tribes revolted and established a rival kingdom under Jeroboam at Shechem. Thus, the history of the people of Israel for the next three and a half centuries is one of two separate kingdoms—Judah in the south (comprising the tribes of Judah and Benjamin) and Israel in the north (containing the other ten tribes). Judah survived until its destruction by the Babylonians in 587 B.C., but Israel disappeared earlier (in 721 B.C.) under an invasion by the Assyrians.

The history of this period is exceedingly complex and, instead of attempting to learn all the details here, the reader will be guided in studying the text by remembering certain basic structures and ideas utilized by the Deuteronomic historians.

1. The Historian's Method. There are two broad divisions in this section. In 1 Kings 12–2 Kings 17 we read an interrelated history of the two kingdoms of Judah and Israel. But since the Northern Kingdom of Israel has been dissolved and the people exiled when we come to the end of 2 Kings 17, the rest of the account in 2 Kings 18–25 is concerned only with Judah. In telling his story of the two kingdoms in 1 Kings 12–2 Kings 17, the historian attempts to help the reader understand events in both by following a regular formula. Concentrating first on the reign of a king in the north or south, the historian then describes events from that king's succession to his death. Then there is a shift to the king or kings who reigned contemporaneously in the other kingdom and a description of the course of events there. Finally the reader is returned to the first kingdom where the story is picked up again. In each reign the historian has an outline: (1) It begins by dating the accession of the king according to the year in the rule of his counterpart in the other kingdom. (2) This is followed by a note regarding the length of his reign. In the case of the kings of Judah, the historian usually includes with this the age of the king at accession and always mentions the name of the queen-mother. With the kings of Israel there is also information about the place of the capital. (3) Then any pertinent incidents in the life of the kingdom are described. (4) Finally the account closes with references to source material for further study and usually to the place of burial and the name of the successor. A good, brief example of this is 1 Kings 15:1-8. There is a great deal of uncertainty about the chronology of this period, since, when added up, the totals of the reigns in the two kingdoms do not agree, or at least do not appear to agree. This is probably reflective of that biblical unconcern with precise dates that we have noted elsewhere.[3]

2. The Historian's Purpose. The historian is writing a theological account of the two kingdoms and so selects and evaluates the material from this perspective. This is why religious, not political, concerns determine the length of discussion. For example, as was previously noted, the reign of Omri of Israel is given only eight verses (1 Kings 16:21-28), while Ahab of Israel is allowed a great deal more (1 Kings 16:29–22:40), even though the former was far more important politically. But because the prophet Elijah was active during Ahab's rule, and because theological emphases were being made, his reign receives extensive treatment. The standard of theological judgment is always the king's loyalty to Yahweh, particularly in reference to idolatrous worship. From this perspective the historian condemns all the kings of Israel, with the exception of Shallum, who reigned only a month (2 Kings 15:13-15). The usual formula of condemnation is: "He did what was evil in the sight of the LORD, and followed the sins of Jeroboam the son of Nebat, which he made Israel to sin; he did not depart from them" (2 Kings 13:2). The author is referring in the phrase "the sins of Jeroboam" to an event at the beginning of the kingdom of Israel. In an attempt to solidify loyalties to the new kingdom, Jeroboam established centers of worship in Israel that would rival Jerusalem. One was at Dan in the north and the other at Bethel in the south. At each of these places he had a golden calf erected as the focus of the worship (1 Kings 12:26-33). These were quite probably not intended by Jeroboam to become idols, but rather to become substitutes for the ark in the temple of Jerusalem. We know that the ark was considered to be the throne of God over which the invisible Lord was manifested. Archaeology also informs us that in pagan worship the comparable animals were considered to be beasts of burden upon which the gods rode. So in Jeroboam's mind worship was intended to be given to the Lord, and the calf became the visible means of directing that worship. But the history of images shows how quickly people forget this careful theological distinction and turn to worship the idol. So it was with the people of northern Israel. Jeroboam's sin was in allowing this distinction to be forgotten so that Israelite worship often became indistinguishable from baalism.

The kings of Judah did not escape the judgment of the historian. With the exception of Hezekiah and Josiah, all southern kings are condemned for their idolatry. Here there is also a common formula: "The high places were not taken away" (1 Kings 15:14). This is a reference to places of worship, usually situated on a hill, where pagan worship was conducted. Israel was commanded to destroy them on entering the land of Canaan (Numbers 33:52; Deuteronomy 33:29), but apparently this was not done, except by Hezekiah (2 Kings 18:4) and Josiah (2 Kings 23:8).

A profound and realistic problem lay behind these simple formulae of condemnation for the kings of Israel and Judah. The failure of the kings to eradicate idolatry was not only a mark of disloyalty to the Lord, but it was also politically disastrous. Hence, the condemnation of the historian and the later prophets was severe. Disloyalty to the Lord meant turning to ways of life that could only mean trouble for the nation. Israel's political and economic security lay in the patterns of life laid down by God. These involved such things as justice and loyalty in family and business. Pagan worship did not encourage these practices but tended to disrupt family and nation.

3. The Kings and Prophets. The story of the divided kingdom revolves around two main figures—king and prophet. This, of course, is in line with the theological purpose of the historian. So not only do we learn of the details of the various kings and their reigns, but also we are given a history of the early prophets. As far as the *kings* are concerned, there was an important difference between kingship in Judah and in Israel. In the south the house of David continued to perpetuate its dynasty throughout the history of the nation, except for the brief reign of Athaliah (2 Kings 11:1-16). Jehoiachin, a Judahite, fell before the first Babylonian onslaught in 597 B.C.; and Zedekiah, another son of Judah, was reigning at the time of the final collapse in 587 B.C. This relative stability was due largely, of course, to the fact that the Southern Kingdom was primarily composed of the tribe of Judah. But another factor was the geographical and political situation. When the northern tribes separated from Judah, the Southern Kingdom was left weak in manpower, natural resources, area, and military ability. Furthermore, Judah was more isolated than the north from trade and international diplomacy. It was easier to maintain a government without foreign intrigues, since Judah was not as attractive a political prize as Israel. But in the Northern Kingdom there was a continual interplay of power factions, and no dynasty was able to establish itself. It had no tradition of a line of kings reaching back to David and Solomon. And thus we read of civil war, assassination, and shift of power in the north.

As far as the *prophets* are concerned, First and Second Kings give dominant attention to two figures—Elijah and Elisha. A few other prophets are mentioned (1 Kings 12:21-24; 13:1-34; 14:1-18; 16:1-4; 20:13-14, 28, 35-43; 22:1-40), and we know from Second Chronicles and the Book of Jeremiah that Jeremiah was very active during the last years of Judah. But Elijah and Elisha are the primary concern of the Deuteronomic historian.

There were two types of prophets throughout the ancient Near East at this time. On the one hand, there was the *nabhi* or "one called" to proclaim a divine message. This title is the one normally translated as "prophet" in the Old Testament. Thus a prophet was a spokesperson, a fact illustrated clearly in Exodus 7:1. Usually found in groups and associated with the temples and shrines of settled areas (1 Samuel 10:5), prophets were characterized more by how they acted than by what they said. They were largely "ecstatics," those who behaved with strange abandon under the influence of music or group psychology and by this indicated the presence of divine power.

In 1 Samuel 10:5-13 Saul is met by a "band of prophets" after he has been anointed by Samuel. These groups were apparently common in Canaan, and Samuel appears to have been the leader of some of them (1 Samuel 19:20). They appear later in the days of Elijah and Elisha under the name "sons of the prophets" (1 Kings 20:35; 2 Kings 2:3, 5, 7, 15). This means simply that they belonged to a class or professional group called "prophets," since the word "son" often carries in the Old Testament the sense of "member of" (see 2 Samuel 7:14, "sons of men").

On the other hand, there was the *roeh* or "one who sees" things hidden to the average person. He was usually the lonely individual who wandered among nomadic or seminomadic groups and was characterized by messages received through visions and dreams. The Israelites received help from a "seer" named Balaam in their fight against the Moabites (Numbers 22–24).

Against this prophetic background we read the stories of Elijah and Elisha, as well as the references to the other prophets. Elijah (1 Kings 17–19; 21; 2 Kings 1) stands more aloof from the sons of the prophets than does Elisha (2 Kings 2–9). Elijah is depicted most of the time as a solitary figure, appearing and disappearing with suddenness. At the great contest against the prophets of Baal on Mount Carmel, Elijah cries: "I, even I only, am left a prophet of the LORD; but Baal's prophets are four hundred and fifty men" (1 Kings 18:22). But Elisha apparently had a group of prophets under his guidance (2 Kings 2:3, 5; 4:38; 6:1). Many of his miracles occurred in a situation where these prophets were present. Both Elijah and Elisha sought to show that Yahweh's will was what affected history, not the desires of the baals. With both prophets, miracles played a large part in demonstrating this assertion, although the miraculous element in the Elisha stories has been heightened by tradition in order to stress Yahweh's effect on events.

In both of these figures we find a type of prophecy that is somewhat different from the prophecy that begins a century later with Amos and Hosea. This does not mean that there is a sharp break, but in reading accounts of the two periods we recognize differences. Elijah and Elisha labored in northern Israel during a period when the future seemed to suggest continued existence in the land of Palestine. Consequently, their view of that future was of growth or decline based on the present situation. Furthermore, their message was directed locally to the rulers of Israel and to the people of the land, and perhaps for this reason tradition has not preserved for us any books by these prophets. Their words were too closely tied to the immediate situation. But the prophets who began with Amos and Hosea saw the future differently. They knew that they stood at the end of an era; the nation was doomed. Chaos would return, although in the distant future restoration would occur. The tone of their message is different; it deals with radical change, and the prophets attempt to prepare the people for this inevitability. Thus these later prophets have a more universal message involving more than Israel; their words have been gathered together into coherent collections. We shall see more of this later.

- How literally is the Deuteronomic view of history to be taken? Does history validate this point of view? Have you ever been troubled about the relation between righteousness and suffering?
- What was the purpose in using the name "Moses" for the collection of laws in Deuteronomy?
- How can we understand the way God works in history? Do the Joshua and Judges accounts help here? Does God directly change events or work more indirectly?
- Why are the Former Prophets called "prophets"? What prophetic lessons do these books proclaim? Can these lessons be illustrated in history?
- Why is Solomon a paradoxical figure? Does this characteristic in Solomon say anything about the kind of person God uses?
- What are some differences between the "miracle" of Joshua 10:6-14 and those illustrated in the lives of Elijah and Elisha? Do miracles still take place?

Additional Resources

Anderson, G. W. *The History and Religion of Israel.* London: Oxford University Press, 1966.

Boling, Robert G., and Wright, Ernest. *Joshua.* The Anchor Bible, vol. 6. Garden City, N.Y.: Doubleday, 1988.

Fretheim, Terence E. *Deuteronomic History.* Nashville: Abingdon Press, 1983.

Gray, John. *Joshua, Judges, and Ruth.* Rev. ed. New Century Bible Commentary. Grand Rapids: William B. Eerdmans, 1986.

Gray, John. *1 and 2 Kings, A Commentary.* 2nd ed. Philadelphia: Westminster Press, 1970.

McCarter, P. Kyle, Jr. *1 Samuel.* The Anchor Bible, vol. 8. Garden City, N.Y.: Doubleday, 1980.

McCarter, P. Kyle, Jr. *2 Samuel.* The Anchor Bible, vol. 9. Garden City, N.Y.: Doubleday, 1984.

Soggin, J. Alberto. *Judges: A Commentary.* Translated by John Bowden. Philadelphia: Westminster Press, 1981.

von Rad, Gerhard. *Deuteronomy: A Commentary.* Philadelphia: Westminster Press, 1966.

3

THE CHRONICLER'S HISTORY

Chronicles–Nehemiah

The third great historical work covers the books of First and Second Chronicles, Ezra, and Nehemiah and traces events from Adam to around 400 B.C. It covers much of the same material found in the Priestly and Deuteronomic Histories; indeed almost one half of the contents of First and Second Chronicles can be found in earlier works. As we shall see, even when the material is repeated, it is used to present a different theological point of view.

INTRODUCTION TO THE CHRONICLER'S HISTORY

In our present Bible the Chronicler's History is broken into four books, but there are clues that tell us that originally there was only one single work of history that embraced all four. In early Hebrew manuscripts, for example, we find that First and Second Chronicles were one book and that Ezra and Nehemiah appeared as one book under the title of Ezra. In addition to this, Chronicles and Ezra-Nehemiah were also joined, as can be seen from the fact that the last two verses of Second Chronicles (36:22-23) are repeated as the first few verses of Ezra (1:1-3). In other words, Second Chronicles ends with an unfinished sentence, which is repeated and completed in Ezra. Quite probably the books were separated, once they were translated, because of their size. Hebrew manuscripts used only consonants and omitted the vowels. But Greek and Latin translations used both, and this, of course, considerably lengthened the books. So in order to make the reading and carrying of scrolls more convenient, the scribes divided the books into separate scrolls. When this was done, some scribe copied the last two verses of Chronicles onto the front of Ezra in order to show the relationship between them. There are other clues as to the original unity of the books. Although now we have two books called Ezra and Nehemiah, the story of Ezra is told in Ezra 7–10 and continued in Nehemiah 8–10, suggesting again an original single book. These facts, plus similarities of style and interest, show that all four books had a single author, whom scholars usually call the "Chronicler."

Because of the general unity of the Chronicler's History, it is usually assumed that the work was written shortly after the last events described in the account, that is, between 400 and 350 B.C. The people of Israel had been back in the land of Palestine for about 150 years. Released from Babylonian slavery by Cyrus the Persian in 538 B.C., the Jews who decided to return had established a precarious existence on the ruins of their homeland. The temple had been rebuilt (515 B.C.), the walls were restored (444 B.C.), and life was taken up again. But at best it was a second-rate existence. The old glory had not returned, although Isaiah had promised them a tremendous future (Isaiah 35). They were still vassals of Persia, desperately poor, with a temple and a city that were only a shabby imitation of those in the days of Solomon. There was often bickering with the other inhabitants of the land. So the questions came: What was their future? Had the exile cut them off from the great promises of the past? In order to show that they were part of the same story of preexilic days, the story of God's purposes being worked out in the world, the Chronicler drew together this material. The purpose was encouragement; the divine promises were still being accomplished, Israel would be central to that fulfillment, and the present did not embrace the full meaning of life. Gerhard von Rad comments: "What can we say about the self-consciousness of a provincial cultic community tolerated by the Persian Empire which yet portrays history from Adam onwards as taking place all for her own sake!"[4]

The Chronicler's method is to take the sources, particularly the Deuteronomic History, and revise, omit, and rearrange to show that the religious community at that time, with its center in the temple at Jerusalem, was the true Israel. It was not the Samaritans, the half-breed Jews who had grown up in Judah during the days of exile, who were God's people. It was the returned exiles. And the key to the Chronicler's argument is the view of the community in worship. The community that was truly God's people was the one that perpetuated a temple worship and priesthood that had been inaugurated by David. The Samaritans were worshiping in different ways than David had commanded, and they had established a rival temple on Mount Gerizim. Therefore, they could not be God's people. So the Chronicler selects and edits the material to speak to the people and to their uncertainty about the fulfillment of the promise. This promise is carried by those who keep worship pure. The point is simple: History is determined by one's attitude toward the worship at Jerusalem. If the present community in Judah wishes to have a future, they must exert all effort to keep the cult pure. This is the kind of work that Yahweh blesses. The speech of King Abijah in 2 Chronicles 13 encapsulates this philosophy. This undergrids the Chronicler's emphasis in tracing the history. David and Solomon, for example, are described as men who established the temple and worship. Ezra and Nehemiah were men who were zealous for keeping that temple and worship pure from foreign contamination.

THE BOOK OF THE CHRONICLES

The Chronicler's purpose comes out clearly when one sees where this history starts. Although beginning with Adam, the whole period from Adam to David is traced only by means of a genealogy in 1 Chronicles 1–9. The Chronicler does not really begin, therefore, until the inauguration of David as king. Notice what has been omitted—the deliverance from Egypt, the wilderness wandering, and the conquest of Palestine, as well as the stories of creation and tales of the patriarchs. The central point of Israel's history in the rest of the Old Testament—the Exodus from Egypt by which Israel was called as God's special people—is ignored. The Chronicler sees the center point as the reigns of David and Solomon and their specific relation to the temple of worship. Here is where the saving relationship with the Lord really begins. It is interesting to notice, as Gerhard von Rad has pointed out, that the

Hebrew verb "to elect" is used by the Chronicler not to refer to the election of Israel, but to the election of David, the temple, and the tribe of Levi (1 Chronicles 15:2; 28:4; 2 Chronicles 7:12, 16; 12:13; 29:11; 33:7).[5] This same point of view can be seen in the concept of "rest." Whereas in Deuteronomy the promise of rest in the land of Palestine is given to all Israel (Deuteronomy 6:10; 7:8; 10:14-15), in Chronicles it is a divine gift for Israel's individual kings (1 Chronicles 22:9; 2 Chronicles 15:15; 20:30).

First Chronicles begins by summarizing the period from Adam to David (1–9) and then deals in detail with the reign of David (10–29). Second Chronicles stresses the reign of Solomon (1–9) and concludes with a survey of the divided kingdom and a brief mention of the release from Babylonian slavery by Cyrus the Persian (10–36). However, the writer utilizes special techniques in describing history. *First,* the Chronicler is obviously interested only in the Southern Kingdom of Judah. The Northern Kingdom apparently is not considered to have been part of the people of God once it broke away after the death of Solomon, for it cut itself off from the temple and true worship at Jerusalem. The northern kings are only mentioned when there was a relationship with a southern king (for example, in 2 Chronicles 18 when Ahab of Israel made an alliance with Jehoshaphat). Also, the Chronicler neglects to note the ministries of Elijah and Elisha or to tell of the fall of the Northern Kingdom in 721 B.C.

Second, the Chronicler idealizes the figures of David and Solomon, and this perspective is in contrast to the rather frank picture in the Deuteronomic History. No real shadow falls on the character of these kings in the depiction of the Chronicler. No mention is made of David's struggle for power, nor of his sordid affair with Bathsheba and Uriah, nor of the humiliation caused by the attempts of Absalom (2 Samuel 14–19) and Adonijah (1 Kings 1–9) to seize the throne. Only the census taking by David is recorded (1 Chronicles 21:1–22:1; 1 Samuel 24), for which the country suffered. But it is intriguing to notice that even here the Chronicler seeks a way out for David by claiming that he was tempted by Satan. David is the perfect king who epitomizes what a king ought to be, particularly in his work of preparing for the building of the temple. David becomes a new Moses in the eyes of the historian.

He was the one who established Israel as it ought to be. Solomon, too, gets this same kind of treatment. Nothing is said about the repressive measures he took in order to gain the throne, or about the idolatry and struggles mentioned in 1 Kings 11. The Chronicler even takes issue with the Deuteronomist on what happened to the twenty cities in the land of Galilee. According to 1 Kings 9:11-12, Solomon had to give them to Hiram of Tyre to pay off a huge debt caused by his building projects. But according to 2 Chronicles 8:1-2, these cities were given by Hiram to Solomon, who then built them into fine cities. One should not say that the Chronicler is trying to whitewash David and Solomon. The Deuteronomic History was well known and these kings' faults were spelled out. The Chronicler wanted rather to concentrate attention on those elements in their reigns that provided the key to their success.

This highly selective character of the Chronicler's writing comes out in the way the kings of the divided kingdom of Judah are handled. Like the Deuteronomic historian, the Chronicler attempts to show that the rules of these kings were dependent upon whether or not they were obedient to the Lord. If they were loyal, they prospered; if they were not, they suffered. But the Chronicler is much more positive that retribution comes immediately upon the sinner and even more clear that the king's relation to the cult was the key. Thus 1 Kings 22:48 says simply that Jehoshaphat of Judah lost some of his ships in a wreck, but 2 Chronicles 20:35-37 claims the shipwreck was due to the fact that Jehoshaphat had allied himself with idolatrous Ahaziah of Israel in the shipbuilding project. Or 2 Kings 15:5 says that the Lord smote Azariah (Uzziah) with leprosy, but 2 Chronicles 26:16-21 adds the explanation that it was because the king had dared to try to burn incense on the altar of incense in the temple. And even murderous Manasseh, who is given heavy-handed treatment in 2 Kings 21:1-18 as one of the worst kings in Judah's history, is described in 2 Chronicles 33:1-20 as having a long rule because he humbled himself before the Lord and cleaned up the worship.

Although an evangelist, the Chronicler was no naive religious enthusiast. The evidence was often overstated and overlooked, but behind this the Chronicler was enunciating a sound view of life.

If worship is truly pure, then all of life is affected, for true worship involves the consideration of God's will in every area of existence. This is the point of Psalms 15 and 24. This emphasis has its dangers. It may develop into legalism and mechanical worship; this indeed is what happened in much of Judaism. It may forget that worship is intended to direct people's eyes to God's sovereignty over all of life.

EZRA-NEHEMIAH

The Chronicler continues the history by means of two biographical accounts; indeed, the story of Nehemiah is basically a personal memoir. The events depicted here give us the only biblical information about the postexilic community in the period between 538 and 400 B.C. The account is not, however, continuous, but describes two main periods in the history of the returned community.

1. The First Phase. In Ezra 1–6 the initial return from Babylonian slavery and the rebuilding of the temple at Jerusalem are described. We saw that in 587 B.C. the Babylonians had captured Jerusalem, destroyed the temple, and carried off many captives to Babylon. Then in 539 B.C. the Persian armies and their allies conquered the Babylonian empire. Cyrus, the Persian general, instituted a remarkably humane policy of allowing the displaced slaves to return to their homelands. There is clear archaeological evidence for this. In Babylon there has been found a baked clay cylinder about nine inches long, containing a record of the exploits of Cyrus. Included in these is mention of his capture of Babylon without a struggle and then an important note that bears on the story in the Book of Ezra. On the cylinder we read: "I [Cyrus] gathered together all their [the cities beyond the Tigris River] inhabitants and restored to them their dwellings." Although this does not mention the Jews by name, this is thoroughly in line with what Ezra reports. In 1:2-4 and 6:3-5 it is recorded that Cyrus not only allowed Jews who wished to do so to return, but also provided financial assistance for the rebuilding of the temple, as well as restoring the temple vessels taken by Nebuchadnezzar. The whole project was placed in the hands of Shesh-bazzar, a member of the royalty. But the majority of Jews did not respond, choosing to remain in Babylonia. Generally pleasant surroundings, opportunities for business advancement, plus the prospect of primitive living conditions in Judah were the factors in their choice. Yet 42,360 Jews did take advantage of the opportunity, and they brought with them around 7500 others (Ezra 2:64-65).

But Judah was not kind to the returning exiles. Plagued by a series of droughts and virtual crop failures (Haggai 1:9-11; 2:15-17), destitute of clothing and food (Haggai 1:6), badgered by the Samaritan occupants of the land, and robbed by others, their enthusiasm soon faded. Work on the temple was suspended (Haggai 2:3; Ezra 4:4-5). But under the leadership of Zerubbabel, the successor of Shesh-bazzar, and Jeshua, the high priest, and with the encouragement of the prophets Haggai and Zechariah, the temple was finally built in 515 B.C. (Ezra 6:13-18).

2. The Second Phase. The story now apparently jumps fifty-seven years to 458 B.C. (Ezra 7–Nehemiah 13). Little is known of the events in the interim period. The community continued to grow, but the walls of Jerusalem, ruined by Nebuchadnezzar's armies, remained in this state. But the chronology is uncertain. Reading Ezra 7, one learns that apparently Ezra came to Jerusalem from Babylon with a group of exiles in the seventh year of Artaxerxes I (464–424 B.C.), the Persian monarch (Ezra 7:7). This would place the time at 458 B.C. Upon arriving, Ezra was disturbed by the lax morals, and he ordered all mixed marriages dissolved (Ezra 7–10). Later we read that Nehemiah arrived on orders from Artaxerxes in the twentieth year of his reign (Nehemiah 2:1), that is, in 444 B.C. In spite of opposition from some Samaritans, he led the people to rebuild the walls in fifty-two days after his arrival (Nehemiah 2–7). Ezra then came and read the Law to the assembled populace, after which all made a covenant with the Lord to follow the precepts of the Law (Nehemiah 8–10). The Book of Nehemiah closes with an account of Nehemiah's return to Babylon and then with his subsequent arrival back in Jerusalem in the thirty-second year of Artaxerxes I, or 432 B.C. (Nehemiah 13:6). At this time he found the morals of the people had again grown lax, so he instituted reform measures, which included divorcing foreign wives.

Most scholars today feel that this outline of events is not the way things actually happened. Most would date Ezra as having followed Nehemiah, but no one is certain when. One of the problems is the fact that the text speaks only of one Persian king as "Artaxerxes," yet we know that there were three Artaxerxes in Persian history. Two of these could fit the period of Ezra and Nehemiah: Artaxerxes I (464–424 B.C.) and Artaxerxes II (404–359 B.C.). But which is which? Some feel that Nehemiah was a cupbearer to Artaxerxes I, while Ezra ministered during the reign of Artaxerxes II. This would mean that Ezra came to Jerusalem in 398, not 458 B.C. Others have placed Ezra in the time of Artaxerxes I but assume that the "seventh year" of Ezra 7:7 is a scribal mistake for the "thirty-seventh year" of Artaxerxes I. This would place Ezra's coming around 428 B.C. The problem is exceedingly complex, and it would not be profitable to examine it in detail here. Suffice it to say that the books of Ezra and Nehemiah are clearly compilations of different kinds of source material—personal memoirs (Nehemiah 1–7, 13), lists (Ezra 2; Nehemiah 7), and official documents (Ezra 1:2-4; 6:3-5). So it would not be inconceivable that some of them became mixed up chronologically in the editing of the books. In fact there is clear evidence of such a thing. Ezra 4:6-23, referring to the time of Ahasuerus (Xerxes, 485–465 B.C.) and Artaxerxes I, is out of place chronologically between 4:1-5 (dealing with Cyrus the Great, 550–530 B.C.) and 4:24–5:17 (speaking of Darius I, 522–486 B.C.).

In all of the descriptions of the work of Ezra and Nehemiah, the Chronicler stresses this theme. Two men are shown who were zealous for keeping the worship of the Lord pure and by this enabled a struggling community to survive and prosper. The Chronicler also emphasizes by the use of genealogy and lists that there is a continuity between the past and the present, in the process providing a balance to the emphasis in the Books of the Chronicles. As we saw, in Chronicles the author ignores the past prior to the days of David. God's work in Israel really begins then with the temple and priesthood. But in Ezra and Nehemiah the author shows us that the importance of the Mosaic days has not been overlooked. The concern is still with cult and worship, but now David is virtually ignored, except for a brief reference to Zerubbabel (Nehemiah 12:46-47). The link with the past is not with David (although his name is not absent), but with Moses. And so the great deeds of the Exodus, the wandering, and the conquest are enumerated by Nehemiah (9:6-37). In a sense, Ezra is seen as another Moses, another lawgiver. His most important move was to gather the entire adult Jewish population in Jerusalem to hear the reading of the Law of Moses, to confess their sins, and to enter into a covenant to keep the Law (Nehemiah 8). The pattern of life for Israel established by Moses in the wilderness was the model for reconstituted Israel under Ezra. Just as Moses had to fight against Baal worship in his camp, so Ezra had to purge out the Samaritan heresy from his own. Thus it was Ezra who set the pattern for the legal community into which Jesus came some centuries later. Israel became a "new community" whose distinguishing mark was not nationality or ethnic background but adherence to a legal formulation that defined the relationship of the people to one another in society and to God.

In their zeal Ezra and Nehemiah show us one of the dangers in laying down patterns of behavior for a community. It can lead to a rejection of outside contributions and to narrowness, bigotry, and pride. But we must not forget that they did preserve the purity of the faith at a time when it could have been lost. If it had been lost, then the community would have disappeared, since it was their peculiar religious beliefs and practices that gave the community coherence and identity.

3. The Samaritan Schism. The rigid rejection of things foreign by Nehemiah and Ezra led to an important event called the "Samaritan Schism." When Nehemiah arrived in Judah, armed with extraordinary powers from Artaxerxes, he met understandable opposition from the leaders already there—Sanballat, governor of the province of Samaria, and Tobiah, governor of the province of Ammon in Transjordan (Nehemiah 2:10; 4:1 and following verses). Both of them were apparently worshipers of the Lord, but their religion had become syncretistic, and thus unacceptable to the purist Nehemiah. Allied with Sanballat and Tobiah was an Arab chieftain named Geshem (Nehemiah 2:19; 6:1, 6), who governed the province of Arabia, a territory which included Edom and southern Judah. Nehemiah was a threat to their authority, and they set about to frustrate his work (Nehemiah 2, 4, 6). But

Nehemiah prevailed, and the walls were built. When Ezra arrived, however, the Samaritan problem flared up and began to worsen. Nehemiah had started it by ejecting Tobiah from the temple and banishing Sanballat's son-in-law from the territory (Nehemiah 13: 28-29). But Ezra's insistence on his interpretations of the Law of Moses and the clear rejection of the Samaritans from temple worship because they were corrupt religiously made the break complete. Sometime after Ezra the Samaritans built their own temple on Mount Gerizim, and from that time onward the Samaritans maintained a rival worship, accepting as authoritative only the Law of Moses.

- What are the differences in the way the Chronicler presents history from the Deuteronomic method? Is there any parallel here with the Gospels?
- How can the Chronicler's veiwpoint be applied to our present world? How does concern for worship today affect our political and social life?
- What lessons do the books of Ezra and Nehemiah give us about the values and dangers of concern over religious purity? What are some specific examples in contemporary life?

Additional Resources

Blenkinsopp, Joseph. *Ezra–Nehemiah: A Commentary.* Philadelphia: Westminster Press, 1988.

Bowman, Raymond A. "The Book of Ezra and the Book of Nehemiah." In *The Interpreter's Bible,* edited by George A. Buttrick et al., vol. 3, 551-819. Nashville: Abingdon Press, 1954.

Myers, Jacob. *1 Chronicles.* The Anchor Bible, vol. 12. Garden City, N.Y.: Doubleday, 1965.

Myers, Jacob. *2 Chronicles.* The Anchor Bible, vol. 13. Garden City, N.Y.: Doubleday, 1965.

Myers, Jacob. *Ezra–Nehemiah.* The Anchor Bible, vol. 14. Garden City, N.Y.: Doubleday, 1965.

4

THE SHORT STORIES

Ruth and Esther

Two little books stand outside the three large historical sections both by form and authorship. They are usually designated as "short stories," not because they are unrelated to actual people and situations, but because they reflect the hand of the artist. Like the stories of the patriarchs, many details have been omitted, the accounts have been simplified, and some aspects are artistic overstatements in order to emphasize certain theological or devotional teachings.

THE BOOK OF RUTH

The story is depicted as taking place in the period of the judges (1200–1020 B.C.) and attempts to show how a poor, foreign widow from Moab was guided by Yahweh and became the great-grandmother of King David. The story is easily followed and artfully told.

What was its purpose? Two basic suggestions have been made. It is usually claimed that the book was written as a protest against the narrow and ruthless attitude of Ezra and Nehemiah in expelling all foreigners from Israel. As we saw, these men were concerned to keep the faith of Yahweh pure and so identified foreigners with foreign religion. But the author of Ruth, living in those postexilic days, took a very old story to protest this too-easy identification of nationality and faith. The faith of Israel had been mixed with foreign blood from the start, for the great King David, founder of Jerusalem worship, had a Moabitess as a great-grandmother. She had shown her loyalty to Yahweh, so the message was clear: Do not reject anyone who wishes to become a believer.

Others have felt that there was another purpose in the book. It is claimed that the two genealogies that close the book (4:17*b,* and 18-22) were later postscripts and could not have entered into the original intent of the author. So the aim of the author was to tell an edifying tale of God's protection of the widow, blessing for loyalty, and guidance for those who trust. The whole account, indeed, moves against a background of the providence of God. Thus the stress would be on the fact that God is present in history, not only in its dramatic events of life, but also in the common experiences of plain people.

The author does not tell the purpose for writing, but simply recounts the moving story. Perhaps both of the ideas suggested above were part of the purpose. The genealogy in 4:18-22 may well have been a later addition, but it seems difficult to think that 4:17 is a postscript. It forms a close part of the story and, in any case, is not the kind of genealogy an Israelite would have invented. David truly did have a Moabite ancestress. Thus it provided the kind of material the author needed to remind the readers in the fifth century B.C. about Yahweh's universal love and care.

THE BOOK OF ESTHER

The inclusion of a book in the canon does not always mean that its teachings or events are examples to be followed. Sometimes we are to read the books for instruction in the frailties of human behavior. This is the case, to a large extent, with the Book of Esther. Here is the story of a beautiful Jewish maiden named Esther who was chosen by the Persian king Ahasuerus (Xerxes; 485–465 B.C.) to be his queen, unaware that she was a Jew. Shortly after she became queen, a severe persecution was instituted by Haman, one of the king's officials, against the Jewish people living in Persia. Esther finally interceded, disclosed that she was a Jewess, and had Haman hanged. At the command of the king, the Jews were then allowed to take revenge on their persecutors. In the capital city of Susa, the Jews killed 810, while in the provinces they slaughtered 75,000. Finally the book closes with the institution of a feast called "Purim," which was intended to commemorate the event of slaughter and deliverance. The word "Purim," by the way, is explained in 3:7 and 9:20-32 as derived from the Persian word "pur" or "lot," the means by which Haman determined the day for his vendetta against the Jews.

The Book of Esther shows us another example of the beautiful way that the Hebrew writers were able to combine historical details with artful embellishments. On the one hand, the author is obviously acquainted with Persian court life and customs (1:6-8, 14; 3:2, 7, 13; 4:2; 5:14; 6:8; 8:10). Information about palace decorations, about customs at banquets, about the names of minor officials, and about the communication of royal edicts has been verified by archaelogical work. On the other hand, the author also includes elements that are not precisely accurate and are intended to be part of the dressing of an interesting story. So the book begins by describing a feast, attended by all the civil and military officials of the Persian empire, that lasted for six months (1:3-4). Later Haman, planning to exterminate all the Jews in Persia (3:5-6), promised the king that, if allowed to carry out his plans, he would pay 10,000 talents of silver into the treasury (3:9). This huge amount would have been equivalent to a major share of the annual revenue of the empire and virtually impossible for Haman to have at his disposal. At the end of the book the great revenge of the Jews over their enemies resulted in the slaughter of 75,000 people in one day, apparently without a loss to themselves.

The book is a highly stylized account of a persecution of Jews in a foreign land. Its language and historical difficulties suggest that it was written some distance removed from the days of Xerxes, probably in the fourth or third centuries B.C. Why was it written? Primarily it came into being in an attempt to provide historical explanation for the celebration of the festival of Purim, since the festival does not appear in the legal texts of the Old Testament. This was particularly needed because the festival had no apparent religious significance. It commemorates the slaughter of Jewish enemies, and although there is a certain underlying sense of divine providence moving through the events, the name of God is not mentioned.

These characteristics—the extreme nationalistic spirit and lack of explicit religious teaching—have caused many to shun the book. There was much debate among the Jews regarding its canonicity, not because of its moral difficulties, but because of the introduction of a new law regarding Purim. According to Leviticus 27:34, the Law of Moses was supposed to be complete. It is common today, when the book is used at all, to see its value for us in showing God's providential care. This is a good evaluation of God, but not of the book. Nothing is really stated about providence, and the whole problem of God's involvement in extreme massacre raises many difficulties if this is assumed as its teaching. Perhaps its religious value for us, if there is any at all, is to show us the results of bitterness and hate. It demonstrates what revenge can do. Fanatically nationalistic and glorifying in an implacable hatred for the enemy, the book pictures for us what happened to the Jews and their call to universal mission. It was one thing to defend themselves against the unjust hatred of Haman. It was another to engage in a ruthless massacre and then to exult in it. The book reminds us that resentment may find many avenues of revenge. Some, like Esther and her people, found one through the slaughter of their enemies. We may simply be more indirect.

Both Ruth and Esther are part of a section in the Jewish canon called the "Megilloth," that is, the Scrolls. This includes five books that although somewhat diverse, have been gathered together because each is read publicly at one of the Jewish festivals. Ruth is read at the feast of Weeks (Pentecost), a time of harvest celebration and historical remembrance (Leviticus 23:15-21). It became specifically a time of remembering the giving of the Law on Mount Sinai, and using Ruth at this time provided a note of universalism. It reminded the Jews of the ultimate purpose of Yahweh for all humanity (Genesis 12:3; Isaiah 2:3). Esther is read, of course, at the festival of Purim, and its purpose we have already seen. The other "Megilloth" are Song of Solomon (Passover), Ecclesiastes (feast of Booths), and Lamentations (feast of Ninth of Ab, which commemorates the destruction of the temple by both the Babylonians (587 B.C.) and the Romans (A.D. 70).

- What are some values of a short story over a historical narrative? How important is the question of historicity to the purpose of the short story?
- How are the attitudes of the people in Ruth and Esther still present in our contemporary racial problems?

Additional Resources

Anderson, Bernhard W. "The Book of Esther." In *The Interpreter's Bible,* edited by George A. Buttrick et al., vol. 3, 823-874. Nashville: Abingdon Press, 1954.

Hubbard, Robert L., Jr. *The Book of Ruth.* The New International Commentary on the Old Testament, vol. 8. Grand Rapids: William B. Eerdmans, 1988.

Moore, Carey A. *Esther.* The Anchor Bible, vol. 7B. Garden City, N.Y.: Doubleday, 1971.

Smith, Louise P. "The Book of Ruth." In *The Interpreter's Bible,* edited by George A. Buttrick et al., vol. 2, 829-852. Nashville: Abingdon Press, 1953.

5

THE SONG TEXTS

Psalms, Song of Songs, Lamentations

The song texts are part of a collection of personal and corporate responses to the events described in the historical and legal texts. This is simply another way of saying that the song literature comes out of the historical period described in the first part of the Old Testament. Most of the time, however, we cannot identify the specific historical situation behind this literature, although many guesses have been made. Part of the continuing value of these books lies in the fact that they are not so closely tied to specific historical events that they reflect situations that will not be repeated. Rather, although we know that the song texts come from the different historical experiences of the Israelites, they are sufficiently vague in their identification of those experiences as to make what they say and how they react typical of situations found in any age.

Strictly speaking, there are two song texts—Psalms and the Song of Solomon. However, I wish also to include Lamentations. Traditionally it has been included in the prophetic books because of assumed authorship by Jeremiah. But it is a poetic lament, not a prophecy, and so it belongs here. We also see that songs are not confined to any particular section in the Old Testament but are scattered all through it (for example, Exodus 15, Habakkuk 3). Actually about 40 percent of the Old Testatment is in poetry, either in the form of a song or as a wisdom saying. But the books of song have been gathered together as a collection because their primary intent is praise or lament or some other form of song expression. The other poetic materials in the Old Testament are part of books or sections whose basic concern is history or prophecy.

THE NATURE OF POETRY

The musical use of poetry has shaped much of its form—brief lines, rhythmic movement, arrangement in patterns. However, there is one primary characteristic that separates Hebrew poetry from prose—parallelism of members or lines. This stylistic device, also found in Babylonia, Canaan, and Egypt, is characterized by the repetition of an idea in successive lines. In other words, a thought will be expressed in one line, and then a second line will convey the same or a related idea in a different manner. Thus, Hebrew poetry does not (except on rare occasions) rhyme word sounds, but rather word ideas.

The simplest unit of Hebrew poetry is the couplet. With this simple unit the Hebrew poet had three basic ways of poetic expression, that is, by means of parallelism. *First,* the poet could use "synonymous parallelism"; in this, the second half of the couplet repeats the thought of the first in a different form and with some variation in meaning. So we read in Psalm 46:7:

> The LORD of hosts is with us;
> the God of Jacob is our refuge.
> (See Psalms 8:3-4; 15:1; 19:1; Job 18:18.)

Second, the poet could employ "antithetic parallelism"; here the second part presents a contrast or antithesis to the first, in order to emphasize the idea of the first line more clearly. So in Psalm 20:8 the psalmist says:

> They will collapse and fall;
> but we shall rise and stand upright.
> (See Psalms 37:9; 55:21; Job 3:3; Proverbs 10:1.)

Third, there is another form, called "synthetic parallelism," in which the second line supplements or completes the thought of the first. Since this is not strictly parallelism, some have rejected it as a category of poetry, calling it "disintegrated parallelism." We hear the psalmist say in Psalm 27:6:

And now my head shall be lifted up
above my enemies round about me.
(See Psalms 3:4; 95:3,5; Job 17:1; Proverbs 26:4.)

Now, of course, most Hebrew poetry is not in the form of a single couplet. A poem is a composition involving a series of couplets, often arranged in unique ways. And so there will be found a wide variety of complex parallel structures. But it should be remembered that no matter how complex the structure may be, it is always composed only of combinations of the three kinds of parallelism shown previously. Thus, for example, Psalm 27 begins with a combination of two synthetic couplets:

The LORD is my light and my salvation;
whom shall I fear?
The LORD is the stronghold of my life;
of whom shall I be afraid?

Or consider how Psalm 51 begins. In verse 1 the first and fourth lines are synthetic to each other, while the second and third are synonymous.

Have mercy on me, O God,
according to thy steadfast love;
according to thy abundant mercy
blot out my transgressions.

Then verse 2, which is clearly part of the initial thought, contains two synonymous lines.

Wash me throughly from my iniquity,
and cleanse me from my sin!

In the structuring of this poem, the Hebrew poet often arranged it so that groups of couplets would be connected by a common idea and would be separated from the lines that preceded or followed. These are called "strophes," from the Greek word for "turning, twisting," a reference to the movement of the chorus in Greek drama in turning to the right or left of the stage. We would call these groupings stanzas or paragraphs. By identifying such groupings we may find clues to the poet's movement of thought. We just saw such a strophe in Psalm 51:1-2. Often these strophes are separated from one another by some device. Sometimes it is a repeated refrain (Psalms 42:5,11; 43:5); at other times the break is made by use of the word "selah" (Psalm 46:3, 7, 11), a word whose meaning is not known.

There are two other characteristics of Hebrew poetry, although prose also contains them to a degree. The first is rhythm. Although it is difficult to capture in translation, often a certain cadence or rhythm can be noticed in reading poetry in Hebrew. And, second, there is a large use of indirect language. Poetry generally gives itself to flights of metaphor and hyperbole. This means that the literalist will not be able to penetrate the meaning of the poem. Poetry expresses its ideas by suggestion and indirection. Thus, one has to feel poetry almost more than read it. When the psalmist cries, "I am reckoned among those who go down to the Pit; I am a man who has no strength" (Psalm 88:4), we recognize that the poet is simply saying what we say in another way which is not far from a literal translation: "I'm in a hell of a spot; I'm dead tired!"

THE PSALMS

Lying at the center of the English Bible and at the heart of worship is the book of Psalms. No other book, even in the New Testament, speaks with such profound and universal language. Here we find expressed the range of moods and experiences through which each of us passes at one time or another. Yet the poetic expression, the cultural metaphors, and the ancient purposes of the various psalms are often confused by the unwary reader. What then is the book of Psalms?

1. A Collection of Religious Poems. The book of Psalms is an anthology of one hundred and fifty poems that arose out of various kinds of situations where religious issues were involved. Some are petitions to God for deliverance from disease or danger; some are praises to God for mercy shown in various ways; some are questions directed to God about such matters as doubt or guidance; some contain snatches of conversation between people; some are virtual monologues or soliloquies. But in all of them we are listening to people expressing themselves in the situations of daily life against the background of faith in Yahweh. Although some of them were deliberate compositions for formal worship, and though all of them came to be used in worship, they are all theological responses to life. But the book of Psalms is not primarily a collection of doctrinal statements about God, although it contains a great amount of doctrine. The psalms are responses to God in light of life's situations where doctrine is confirmed or apparently denied.

Scholarship has, in relatively recent days, tended to classify the poems in the book of Psalms according to basic types, and this classification has given us great help in reading what is intended in the particular psalms. It is usually impossible to determine the specific historical situation behind each psalm, since historical allusions are few, and the titles are indefinite or unreliable. So scholars now classify the psalms according to the *kind* of historical and religious situation and leave unanswered the actual historical background. There is no agreed-upon classification scheme today, and some psalms are mixtures of types (19, 90, 119). The following sixfold scheme is representative of one approach at embracing the different types in the book, each of which is representative of a different kind of religious setting:

a. *Hymns of praise.* These contain expressions of praise for various aspects of God's character and work. Sometimes they praise God for goodness and greatness in general (111, 113, 115, 117, 145–150); some emphasize the greatness of God displayed in the natural process (8; 19:1-6, 29); others speak of God's lordship over the nations (47, 93, 95–99); and others praise Zion as the dwelling place of God (46, 66, 84, 87, 122).

b. *Prayers in time of trouble.* Here we read petitions to God regarding threat of invasion, bodily suffering, natural calamity, deceitful friends, and so on. Songs of this type are the most numerous in the book. Some are individual laments, using the vivid language of hyperbole and metaphor reflective of the difficult situation (5, 22, 42, 51, 69, 88). Others are communal laments dealing with threats to the nation or the community (44, 60, 74, 79, 83, 85).

c. *Songs of thanksgiving and trust.* These psalms are expressions of thanksgiving related to particular favors granted by God. They often reflect the result of answers to prayer in time of trouble. Again, some are individual songs (23, 27, 73, 116, 118, 121), and others are communal songs (48, 65, 67, 75, 100, 124).

d. *Psalms for liturgical worship.* A few psalms within the book give indication of being liturgies for particular festivals. They often have antiphonal elements in which the choir and the priest, and perhaps the worshipers, took part (14 [or 53], 15, 24, 50, 81, 82, 95).

e. *Wisdom songs.* The purpose of some of the psalms appears to be primarily didactic; that is, they present teachings regarding proper ways of living. The particular emphasis of these is the contrast between righteous and unrighteous living. Sometimes they are lengthy discussions on a basic theme (1, 37, 139), and at other times they are collections of short maxims (112, 127, 128, 133).

f. *Psalms of royalty.* The Old Testament gives abundant evidence that the reigning king had a particularly central role in the worship of Israel (for example, 1 Samuel 26:11; 1 Kings 3:4). So it is not surprising that different events in the life of the king were celebrated in song at the temple. Characteristic of this type is the magniloquent language used to refer to the monarch, so that he may even be called God's "son" (2:7) or even "God" (45:7). The following occasions can be seen: the enthronement ceremonies (2, 101, 110), the anniversary of such an event or the king's birthday (21, 72), the anniversary of the founding of the Davidic dynasty (132), a royal wedding (45), the departure for battle (20; 144:1-11), and the victorious return from battle (18). Some of these have traditionally been thought to be "messianic," that is, predictions of the Messiah. However, originally these songs were expressions of kingly ideals that were unfulfilled in the ruling king, and so they became used as means of expressing Israel's expectations or hopes for the Messiah (see 2:7 and Acts 13:33).

2. A Hymnal for Worship. Originally many of the psalms undoubtedly came from nonformal worship situations in the palace, the city-gate, the home, and the field (for example Psalms 42, 43, 51). Yet all of them probably were used in formal worship at different times. In any case, the form in which we now have the psalms served as a hymnal to be used for public and private worship. They were intended to be chanted or sung. This can be determined by various clues. First, there is the name of the book—

The Psalms. It comes from the Greek word *psalmos,* "music of a stringed instrument"; this then developed to mean "a song sung to the accompaniment of a stringed instrument." The book is also called the "Psalter." This is the Greek *psalterion,* "stringed instrument" or "psaltery"; again the word developed to mean "songs sung to the accompaniment of a psaltery." In the Hebrew Bible the book is called *Praises.* This is derived from the fact that a dominant element of the book is praise to God. Second, the hymnal character is shown by the various titles that give musical directions and directions for worship. Psalm 100 is accompanied by a note that says it was used to accompany a "thank offering." A note on Psalm 4 is "to the choirmaster; with stringed instruments." At what date these titles were added is difficult to say, but they appear to have been collected for use in worship.

When it is stated that the book of Psalms is a hymnal for worship, this does not mean that it could not have had other uses. Some feel that it also was used as a wisdom collection. In other words, because some of the psalms do not fit the worship situation too well, or at least are rather didactic, perhaps those who collected the psalms intended them also to be employed in the schools of wisdom for instruction in Israel's religion or for guidance in daily life. This would be the case, for example, with Psalms 1, 37, 112, and 127. Although this may be correct, we must not exclude the possibility that worship in Israel could also incorporate wisdom instruction. This may be indicated by the title to Psalm 89, which is clearly intended for singing in worship. The title reads "A Maskil of Ethan the Ezrahite"; the word "maskil" probably means "wise advice."

3. A Limited Collection. It is clear that all of Israel's psalms were not put into the Psalter. It is simply a limited collection of 150 psalms out of a wide range of Israelite poetry. This can be seen from the fact that not only does one find psalms elsewhere in the Old Testament (Jonah 2, Isaiah 38:9-20; Habakkuk 3; Exodus 15), but also among the Dead Sea Scrolls and other Jewish writings.

The ancient Greek translation, the Septuagint, actually has 151 psalms in its collection of the Psalter, and it labels the last one "outside the number." Among the Dead Sea Scrolls is a copy of this 151st psalm, along with further additions to the book of

Psalms. This practice of selecting and adapting hymns is still the practice for worship. Many church groups have their own *Selected Hymns of the Faith,* or a collection will be published with some such title as *One Hundred Favorite Gospel Songs.*

4. An Arranged Collection. The hand of the editor can be seen in the ways that the separate psalms have been brought together according to various arrangements. The whole book of Psalms is divided into five parts of unequal length. Each part ends with a doxology, and then the whole book ends with the last psalm itself being a doxology (1–41, 42–72, 73–89, 90–106, 107–150). As George S. Gunn comments: "The position of Psalm 150 is no more an accident than that of Psalm 1. It is hard to imagine any appropriate alternative way in which the Psalter could have been brought to a close. Any other conclusion would have been an anticlimax indeed."[6] This grand fivefold arrangement is generally assumed to be in imitation of the Pentateuch. So this time we are given a Pentateuch associated with David's name, whereas the first was related to Moses.

THE SONG OF SONGS

This book illustrates graphically the fact that the Old Testament speaks to all areas of human life. Here we find an anthology of love songs, most of which were sung at weddings in the ancient Near East, in which bride, groom, and wedding guests all participate to extol the glories of love. In a word, the book proclaims that the sexual relationship between a man and a woman is to be enjoyed openly and thankfully, but responsibly.

The title in most English translations is "The Song of Solomon." This is simply an abbreviation of the Hebrew words of 1:1: "The Song of Songs, which is Solomon's." The phrase "Song of Songs" is the Hebrew way of expressing the superlative and thus means "the finest, loveliest, best song." This expresses the mood of the book better than the flat "Song of Solomon" (see 8:6-7). Sometimes the book is called "Canticles" (Songs), a name derived from the Latin or Vulgate version title "Canticum Canticorum" (Song of Songs).

An understanding of its literary character is crucial to reading the book, but this has been very much debated in the history of the church. Most are agreed that it is poetry, and thus obviously the literalist will miss much of the meaning (for example, 4:4, 5:14). But what kind of poetry does the book contain? There have been two basic approaches.

1. A Unified Treatise. Historically most interpreters have seen the book as a unified poem of some sort. One popular view has been that the book is an *allegory* depicting God's love for God's people. It was because of this interpretation that the book was finally accepted in the canon. From earliest times Jewish interpreters have seen two main figures in the book—Solomon and his bride, the Shulammite maiden. These were thought to be allegorical for God and Israel, and so the book was interpreted as depicting in detail God's love for the people of God. This accounts for the use of the Song of Songs at Passover, for this event demonstrated God's great love for Israel. The Christian church took over this interpretation and baptized it to teach the relationship between Jesus Christ and his church. The prevalence of this approach can be seen by the comments often printed at the top of the columns of text in the King James Version. It is also this interpretational view that has provided imagery for many hymns—"I Come to the Garden Alone," "Majestic Sweetness Sits Enthroned," "Fairest Lord Jesus," and others.

Another popular view has taken the book to be either a *drama* or a *parable,* that is, a connected play or story teaching some particular moral lesson. The difference between this and the allegorical interpretation lies basically in the fact that it concentrates only on the broad outlines of the story, and it does not try to find meaning in all the details. Some have maintained that the book describes the story of Solomon's love for a country girl and tells how with her he finds a love more profound than he has for any other harem maiden. Thus, the book teaches God's special love for God's people. Others find three principal characters in the book—Solomon, the Shulammite maiden, and her shepherd lover. Here Solomon is attracted by the country girl, takes her off to the palace, and tries to woo her. But she remains true to her shepherd lover. The point is then to show faithful believers that they should remain true to their commitment to God in spite of worldly temptations.

So one can see that the problem of its literary character is difficult. Yet there has come increasing evidence that neither the allegorical nor the dramatic/parabolic approach is correct. There are no clues in the book that suggest we are to read it for other than what it appears to be—a loose collection of love songs. But where were these songs used?

2. A Loosely Arranged Collection. Because of the very erotic imagery that finds many parallels in the pagan worship of that day, some scholars believe that the book is a collection of *liturgical songs.* As we have seen, Israel lived in the midst of a culture where worship was closely connected with fertility rites, and the book is filled with symbolism that reflects this—doves, pomegranates, apples, and so on. So it has been proposed that the two lovers are to be interpreted as a god and a goddess. The songs were, therefore, used in Israel's worship as accompaniment and direction for two actors who mimicked in worship the supposed actions of the gods. But fertility worship was so frequently denounced by the prophets that it is difficult to see how the book, if it were really a collection of pagan fertility songs, could have been venerated in Israel.

The interpretation that seems most natural is one that sees the book to be a collection of *love and wedding songs.* In the ancient East, weddings were celebrated with a succession of feasts, at which the bride and groom sang songs extolling the beauty of each other. They were spoken of as "king" and "queen," and dances were performed by and for them (see 3:9, 7:1). This interpretation would explain why then throughout the book the bridegroom is called "Solomon" and the bride is "the Shulammite." Solomon was Israel's most glorious king, and the Shulammite maiden was renowned for her beauty and appeal (1 Kings 1:3; 2:17). Thus, these are titles for the couple and not references to the actual Israelite king and his bride. They are stylistic devices of Hebrew love songs to refer to the bridegroom and bride. This then shows that Solomon was not the author; indeed, the implied condemnation of polygamy in 6:8-9 and 8:11-12 is further evidence that he was not.

One should, therefore, read the book with appreciation for its frank, love-song expression, recognizing that it is poetry, and accepting the fact that it comes from a time and culture when images were earthy and direct. In these songs of pure, passionate, sexual, hungry love there is sounded a note of enjoyment of the created relationship between man and woman. But this is coupled with a sense of responsibility for loyalty and exclusiveness in the commitment of love. There is no outline to the book; it is an anthology of twenty or so separate songs or parts of songs, all of which deal with the common theme of love. A good translation that separates the various songs or poems will aid in reading.

THE LAMENTATIONS OF JEREMIAH

This collection of poems expresses a theme quite opposite to that of the Song of Songs. This is a series of songs of lamentation all dealing with the destruction of Jerusalem by the Babylonian armies in 597 and 587 B.C. and written sometime shortly after this event. They mourn the suffering and desolation; they confess Israel's sins that brought this about; but they also look to the future when restoration will take place.

The name of the book in English comes from the Greek and Latin versions, and an early Jewish tradition gives it the same name. Most Hebrew manuscripts and printed editions, however, title the book by the first word of chapters 1, 2, and 4—"How." The full English title is "The Lamentations of Jeremiah," but the book itself does not give any definite clue as to authorship. The identification of the book with Jeremiah comes first from the Greek Bible in the second century B.C. and was perhaps suggested by 2 Chronicles 35:25. That Jeremiah could have written the poems is possible, but not certain. All of the songs were apparently composed by one person, for they show similarities in style and content. Yet most scholars follow the Jewish tradition that separated the book from Jeremiah and leave the question of authorship unsolved.

It is readily apparent that the book is a collection of five separate songs or poems, each of which comprises a chapter. In general, they are all funeral laments, some predominantly of an individual nature (chapter 3); others express community feelings (chapter 5); and others are a mixture. If there was a single author, this may be evidence of oscillation between personal anguish and a sense of solidarity with the sufferings of the nation. In any case, the author intends the personal feelings and questions to be expressions of corporate response to the tragic situation. The author describes in graphic detail the terrible carnage wrought by the enemy soldiers, the children dying from hunger and disease, the futility of the leadership, and the cessation of worship. And so the writer asks in essence: What is the significance of these dark days? What part did the Lord play in them? What is the future of Israel? On the one hand, the author answers by confessing that Israel deserved the disaster because of its sins, and thus it is a judgment from God (see especially 1–2, 4–5). On the other hand, the author expresses confidence that God has not deserted Israel, and thus there is hope for the future (see chapter 3).

- How are the various poetic parallel forms illustrated in Psalms 23 and 51?
- What experiences and attitudes in modern life are reflected in Psalm 69? What is Psalm 15 expressing about the relationship between faith and life? Give specific illustrations in your present church and community.
- What lessons about the relationship between man and woman are there in the Song of Solomon? How is love demonstrated?

Additional Resources

Anderson, A. A. *Psalms, Volume 1 (1–71).* New Century Bible Commentary. Grand Rapids: William B. Eerdmans, 1981.

Anderson, A. A. *Psalms, Volume 2 (73–150).* New Century Bible Commentary. Grand Rapids: William B. Eerdmans, 1981.

Anderson, Bernhard W. *Out of the Depths: The Psalms Speak for Us Today.* Philadelphia: Westminster Press, 1983.

Hillers, Delbert R. *Lamentations.* The Anchor Bible, vol. 7A. Garden City, N.Y.: Doubleday, 1972.

Lewis, C. S. *Reflections on the Psalms.* New York: Harcourt, Brace & World, 1958.

Meek, Theophile J. "The Song of Songs." In *The Interpreter's Bible,* edited by George A. Buttrick et al., vol. 5, 91-148. Nashville: Abingdon Press, 1956.

Pope, Marvin H. *Song of Songs.* The Anchor Bible, vol. 7C. Garden City, N.Y.: Doubleday, 1977.

Weiser, Artur. *The Psalms: A Commentary.* Philadelphia: Westminster Press, 1962.

6

THE WISDOM TEXTS

Job, Proverbs, Ecclesiastes

Human beings from the earliest times have been searching for the good life, the best way to live. The biblical wisdom literature claims to provide instruction in finding this kind of life, particularly in reference to day-to-day experiences. Most of the time this wisdom is given through poetry, so that these books share with the song texts a poetic form (except for prose sections like Job 1–2 and 42:7-17), often using the same forms of parallelism that are found in the songs. Thus, the material is to be read imaginatively and loosely. This literature found its place in school and family situations, and perhaps also in worship.

THE NATURE OF WISDOM LITERATURE

The term "wisdom," perhaps from the root idea of "firmness," is the general expression for the knowledge of how to do things, or how to get along in life. Someone has called it "the art of success." Therefore, this literature always has a practical, rather than a theoretical, purpose. It deals with living life to its fullest by learning such things as how to live with others, how to handle one's money, how to do certain tasks skillfully, or how to understand the basic issues of life. On the one hand, it can refer to some *utilitarian ability.* A tailor is a "wise" person (Exodus 28:3) as is a carpenter (Exodus 31:6-7) or a government official (2 Samuel 14:20). Each of these persons has "wisdom" because each knows how to work skillfully. On the other hand, wisdom has a *theological quality.* This aspect is the dominant characteristic of the wisdom literature, which is concerned with the meaning of life under God. Questions about the purpose of life and the presence of evil in the world are the kinds of questions with which wisdom literature deals. But even in these cases one can see that wisdom is practical in that it seeks to help a person find the way to a good life. The point that wisdom literature makes is always that the good life is attained only when one follows God's ways, as epitomized in Proverbs 2:6: "The LORD gives wisdom; from his mouth comes knowledge and understanding." Or Job asks: "Where shall wisdom be found? And where is the place of understanding? Man does not know the way to it, and it is not found in the land of the living" (Job 28:12-13). Job answers his own question: "God understands the way to it, and he knows its place" (Job 28:23).

Wisdom, of course, is not restricted to the Old Testament. The wise saying was a favorite form by which Jesus taught (Matthew 5). In this regard he is even described as "greater than Solomon" (Matthew 12:42). That Paul calls Christ "the wisdom of God" (1 Corinthians 1:24) has an interesting background in Proverbs 8 where wisdom is personified.

Other than the Bible there is also a vast body of wisdom literature. The Jews had a number of books that never got into the canon, and archaeologists have discovered great volumes of similar literature from Egypt, Babylonia, and Canaan. Many times this material is similar to that in the Old Testament. We must remember that Israel was influenced by the cultures of these nations with which it traded. We know that many laws were adopted from these places, and we have seen that the major festivals of Israel were adaptations of Canaanite feasts. The temple of Solomon was modeled along Phoenician and Egyptian lines. Thus, it is not strange that proverbs from Israel show similarities as well, particularly since the stress of everyday life and its problems is common to any people. The most striking illustration of this similarity is Proverbs 22:17–23:14, which seems to have been adapted from the Egyptian wisdom book called *The Teachings of Amenemope* (1000–600 B.C.). There are differences, of course, such as: biblical wisdom is monotheistic; there is only one God, Yahweh. Also, the motivation for wise behavior is usually different. Although following the wise way is certainly motivated by self-interest, since the biblical writers are careful to stress that wisdom is the divine way for humans to live, one follows the precepts of wisdom as a means of response to the Lord. Hence, Old Testament wisdom must always be seen against the background of the convenant relationship. If Israelites committed themselves to the Lord, then one proof of that commitment was the way they took Yahweh's will seriously in everyday life.

THE BOOK OF JOB

One of life's problems that has continued to badger the minds of people through the centuries concerns the reason for suffering. Sometimes suffering is understandable because we bring it upon ourselves. But often tragedy strikes apparently innocent people. This then raises the wider problem of the character of God. Why is this world so disordered if there is a God? Or what kind of God do we worship? Maybe there is no God at all. It is because these questions have gone unanswered that countless men and women have floundered in their faith. The Book of Job speaks to this agonizing problem. As part of the wisdom literature, it attempts to solve the problem of how to get along in a world that seems so wrong so many times. It is basically the story of a man who sought to find meaning in life while going through a series of terrible physical, mental, and spiritual sufferings. So although the apparent question of the book is "Why am I suffering?" the real question it is attempting to answer is "How can a person have faith in God in such a mixed-up world?" Suffering is only the vehicle by which the wider question of faith is raised.

The heart of the book is an involved series of poetic dialogues and monologues (3:1–42:6) surrounded by a prose narrative prologue (1:1–2:13) and epilogue (42:7-17). The prologue sets the scene. A man named Job, extremely wealthy and genuinely pious, is struck down by a series of tragedies. He loses his wealth, his children, and his health. Unknown to him these losses have been caused by Satan, and ultimately by God. God had boasted to the heavenly court about Job's goodness, but Satan had doubted Job's motives for his goodness. Satan felt that Job served God because it paid off. So the Lord had allowed Satan to test Job's faithfulness.

But Job refuses to turn against God, and Satan disappears from the scene. However, this is only the start of the book, for Job's tragedies have not been reversed. As three old friends come to comfort Job in his agony, their visit becomes the occasion for the long series of poetic dialogues and monologues. The purpose of these dialogues is to probe the cause of Job's suffering and thus to find the basis for faith in God.

The first group of speeches (3–31) contains a series of dialogues between Job and his three old friends. Actually, it is a series in three cycles (3–14, 15–21, 22–31). First, Job speaks, and then his friend Eliphaz responds. Next, Job speaks again, and the second friend, Bildad, replies. Job then answers him, and the third friend, Zophar, speaks. After Job has answered Zophar, the whole cycle starts over to go its round two more times. Actually Zophar's third speech is missing, although it is possible that it comprises 27:13-23 and the title has simply been lost in the process of copying. Job's beginning speech in chapter 3 is really a soliloquy of agony, in which he wonders about the faith by which he has lived his life. He questions why he was born (3:3-10), why he has to live (3:11-19), and why he cannot now die (3:20-26). Job realizes that he is not the only innocent sufferer. He raises the wider problem of all sufferers by using the plural "bitter ones in soul, who long for death" (3:20-21). It must be remembered that Job and his friends know nothing about the conversations between the Lord and Satan. In the long series of dialogues with Job, his friends have one simple solution, which they hammer at over and over again. Suffering comes because of sin, so Job must have sinned. If Job will repent, his suffering will cease. This note is sounded right off in Eliphaz' first speech (4:7-9). But Job consistently refuses to accept this advice, for he knows from his own life and from observing others that suffering is not always a guarantee that sin is the cause. This is his problem: He is not a sinner (9:15), yet God seems to be responsible for his condition (6:3-4). Job wonders if something has happened to God, and so he ends the series of speeches with a challenge to God to face him honestly and to explain what is going on (31:35-37).

The second group of speeches (32–37) is basically a monologue by a fourth friend named Elihu. Job does not respond to him. Elihu does not contradict the three friends in their claim that the sufferer is always a sinner. He simply approaches it from the other side. The friends have taken a negative approach—Job is being punished. But Elihu takes a positive tack—God is disciplining Job. Affliction is sent by a God of love in order to discipline and purify, and thus to save a person from premature death (see 33:1-33).

The third group of speeches (38:1–42:6) is a dialogue between Job and the Lord. But the appearance of the Lord is a bit puzzling. God makes no reference to Job's problem or to his friends, but merely reveals the divine being as all-powerful, all-wise, all-loving. The point God is making is thus: Human beings must not question God, not because humans are to remain unthinking, but because life is too complex for their understanding. Only God understands completely, and humans can rest assured that God cares and is lovingly at work in the world. Therefore, people must submit to God because they cannot save themselves or understand the world. God speaks twice, and Job responds twice. In 38:1–40:2 God addresses Job's wisdom. Showing him the vastness of creation, God implies that human wisdom is limited and cannot understand all the reasons for life. Job responds in 40:3-5 with a confession of humility. In 40:6–41:34 God speaks to Job's power. People's inability to rule the universe makes them unable to judge God's actions. Here God asks Job sarcastically: If you can do it any better, why don't you try? But Job knows he cannot. The point is simply that if God knows and cares for the world of nature, how much more must God be concerned about humans, about Job! So Job responds in 42:1-6 with an affirmation of trust in God.

The book comes to a conclusion in the prose epilogue (42:7-17). Job's misfortune is reversed, and Job's friends are rebuked for their bad advice. With the conclusion comes the basic theological point of the book. At the beginning the author had, in essence, raised the question: "Can a person have faith in God in such a mixed-up world?" The friend had answered: "Certainly, for the world is *not* mixed-up. All sufferers are sinners." But neither Job nor we can accept this, as God has revealed. The Lord answers: "Yes, for although the world is in a mess, I still have loving reasons. All sufferers are not sinners." So Job comes to a faith that all the vicissitudes of life are known and cared for by a loving, sovereign

God. Innocent people like Job may suffer, but God can still be trusted. Here is justification by faith, not by knowledge or works.

The book has its problems, and some of them spring out of its composition. Like all Old Testament books this one is a composite. The main problem concerns the prologue and epilogue. Theologically they teach that God tempts humans, but this interpretation conflicts with the teaching in James 1:13. Literally their conceptual differences with the poetic section seem to suggest different origins. Therefore, many scholars feel that the really creative part of the book is found in the poetic section, and the prose prologue and epilogue are part of the source material utilized by the author. In other words, it is felt that the prologue and epilogue were an ancient story about a man named Job. A traditional, pious point of view about God and humanity's response to God was reflected in this popular story. God was a sovereign despot who could control humans, and humanity's response was simply to give absolute, unquestioning submission: "The LORD gave, the LORD has taken away; blessed be the name of the LORD" (Job 1:21). But the author of Job was unable to accept this kind of faith, or rather this blind obedience, and needed some reasons for faith. So the author borrowed the old story and used it as a framework and foil for this spiritual search. The ancient account dealing with a "patient Job" (1:1–2:10; 42:11-17) was taken and retold and supplemented with transitional material (2:11-13; 42:7-10) in the form of poetic dialogues about a "protesting Job." (3:1–42:6). Thus the author was making a personal protest against a false view of God, reflected in the prologue and epilogue, that had developed among the people. The God who emerges out of the poetic dialogues of 38–42 is a far cry from the God who wagers with Satan in the prose prologue and pays off Job in the epilogue.

This view means, therefore, that the Book of Job is not history; indeed, we do not know how much of the book is based on real individuals and events. Ezekial 14:14, 20 reflect a knowledge in Israel of the story of an ancient righteous man named Job. Probably the book should be viewed in the same light as Jesus' parable of the good Samaritan or of Lazarus in Abraham's bosom. These were real individuals, but they now appear in stories that are the product of the literary artist. Their purpose is not history, but theology, and they have been stylized and shaped to this end. The beautiful poetic dialogues are clearly the product of literary craftsmanship and not of spontaneous conversation. The exact date the Book of Job was written is unknown. Probably it comes from the postexilic days in Israel (sixth to fifth centuries B.C.), when wisdom teaching was in the air and when the problem of faith had become particularly acute after the destruction of the nation.

THE PROVERBS

One of humanity's basic needs is the ability to live harmoniously with other people. The book of Proverbs seeks to provide a guide to such living. It surveys a host of situations in everyday life, and it suggests what is right and wrong conduct in each of them, what patterns of behavior will bring joy and success, and what ways of life are destructive. Jesus pointed out that the law of love—love of God and love of neighbor as oneself—was the sum of the Old Testament (Mark 12:29-31). The book of Proverbs gives us a series of examples of what this love means in practice.

What is a proverb? The Hebrew word for "proverb" *(mashal)* covers a wide range of forms. It is apparently derived from the root idea "to represent, be like." Thus, it is used basically to describe a brief "comparison" or "representation," that is, a description not relating only to a single fact but "representing" other similar facts. For example, Proverbs 10:26 reads: "Like vinegar to the teeth, and smoke to the eyes, so is the sluggard to those who send him." Here the comparison is clear. However, the word *proverb* developed to include more than strict comparisons. It is used of a simple folk-saying (for example, 1 Samuel 10:12) or a lengthy discourse (for example, Isaiah 14:4-21). In the book of Proverbs two types are used. The more common is the short maxim, often in the form of direct advice (for example, 19:18), but many times it is simply an observation of life (for example, 17:17). The other type is the lengthy discourse or vignette in which the lesson is not stated directly, but it is intended to be inferred by the hearer or reader (for example, 7:1-27).

The composite character of biblical literature is amply illustrated here, for Proverbs is a collection of collections from various people and groups. This can be seen not only from the disparate nature of the contents, but also from the headings of various sections (1:1; 10:1; 24:23; 25:1; 30:1; 31:1). So when the book begins with these words: "The proverbs of Solomon, son of David, king of Israel" (1:1), we are not to understand them as an ascription of authorship, but as an indication that Solomon was responsible for the particular collection that follows. The date of the present book is therefore quite different from the date of its contents. The final editing was probably around the fifth or fourth century B.C. But since proverb materials contain the distillation of Israel's experience, they are gleaned from many centuries. There are even non-Israelite sayings in the book, such as in 22:17–23:14, which show a striking resemblance to some Egyptian proverbs from the text *The Teachings of Amenemope,* dated between 1000 and 600 B.C. Yet on these Israel has placed its particular theological stamp. Amenemope advises:

> Guard yourself against robbing the wretched,
> and against being forceful over the helpless (2:1-2)

But the author of Proverbs 22:22-23 writes:

> Do not rob the poor, because he is poor,
> or crush the afflicted at the gate;
> for the LORD will plead their cause
> and despoil of life those who despoil them.

The purpose of Proverbs. As a guide to successful living, the purpose is spelled out in 1:2-6. Here such words as "wisdom," "instruction," "knowledge," and "words of insight" are to be understood as referring to the contents of the proverbs in the rest of the book. It is to be noticed that 1:2 begins by saying "that men may know wisdom and instruction," and then the context goes on to span the range of people from the "simple" (1:4) to the "wise" (1:5). The word "simple" is here a synonym for "youth"; that is, it does not refer to one who is simple-minded, but to one whose knowledge is still at the elementary stage. Yet the book is also intended for the "wise," suggestive of the point that one is never too old to learn. Behind the teaching, however, directed at different classes of people lies a foundational idea that is the theme of all wisdom teaching in the Old Testament. It is expressed in 1:7: "The fear of the LORD is the beginning of knowledge; fools despise wisdom and instruction." This means, first, that not only the first in time but also the most essential thing to learn is to fear the Lord. But, second, the word "fear" must not be misunderstood. It is not simply a cringing, fawning dread. It speaks to a right state of heart and life toward God. It means taking God into account as the sovereign Lord of this world. Perhaps it is better translated as "reverence." This is why Isaiah 11:3 can speak of having "delight" in the fear of the Lord. When we respect the will of the one who rules the world and who has established patterns of life that will bring lasting joy, then it truly is a "delight."

ECCLESIASTES

This strange book speaks to a universal human problem—the search for meaning in life. In this respect it is similar to the Book of Job, but its conclusion is radically different. Job had proclaimed trust in a purposeful, loving, albeit mysterious, God. But the author of Ecclesiastes saw God only as enigmatic and mysterious. Forget God and trust in the moment; that is all that is real and dependable.

The key to reading the book is found in the recurring phrase "under the sun"—"What does man gain by all the toil at which he toils under the sun?" (1:3)—that is, during your lifetime from your human viewpoint. These words keep appearing in the book and give us the perspective from which all of the author's advice proceeds. The author assumes, unlike the rest of the Old Testament (except for Proverbs 30:1-4), that God is unknowable and unrelated to humanity. There is no communication from the divine (3:11). Therefore, one has to search for life's meaning and goals by oneself, by things "under the sun." So the highest good in life consists in accepting this fact and in enjoying the relationships and elements of life that one can while one can enjoy them. The author is thus a philosopher, not a theologian, not denying the existence of God, but only denying that God's ways and purposes can be determined by humans.

Who was this agnostic? The author tells us that he was a professional wise man and teacher (12:9). His youth had slipped away, and he was approaching old age (11:9–12:7). But much more than this we cannot know.

The author was not Solomon, although traditionally he has been identified with the "son of David" (1:1). The lateness of language and comments regarding kingship (4:13; 8:2; 9:14-16; 10:16-17, 20) have led most scholars to conclude that an unknown author of the fourth or third century B.C. used the "king" as a literary device for these wisdom speculations. We call the author the "Preacher," a translation of the Hebrew participle "Koheleth," which probably means "one who assembles a group" (1:1). The English title "Ecclesiastes" comes from the Greek attempt to translate "Koheleth." "Ecclesiastes" in Greek means "member of an assembly." The structure of the book is loose without any coherent sequence of argument. It contains a series of autobiographical reflections, admonitions, and proverbial sayings.

1. The Basic Problem of Life (1:2-11). When all is said and done, life is empty, frustrating, and meaningless. This is summed up in the opening words: "Vanity of vanities, says the Preacher, vanity of vanities! All is vanity" (1:2). The word "vanity" means literally "breath" (Isaiah 57:13) or "vapor" (Proverbs 21:6), and so it is a figure for something that is visible, but worthless and temporary. This is why the author adds: "What does man gain by all the toil at which he toils under the sun?" (1:3). The answer is—nothing, because life is one endless, meaningless repetition with no goal. There is movement everywhere, but nothing really changes or advances (1:4-11).

2. The Evidence of Life's Failure (1:12–2:23; 3:1–4:16; 5:8–6:12; 8:10-14). The author surveys the various areas of life and shows how each fails to provide ingredients to make human life ultimately worthwhile and fulfilling—education (1:12-18), pleasure (2:1-11), the incongruity of life (2:12-17; 4:1-3; 6:10-12; 8:10-14), work (2:18-23; 4:4-6), religion (3:1-15), the lack of immortality (3:16-22), wealth (4:7-12; 5:8-20; 6:1-9), and popularity (4:13-16). The dominant note is that all of human endeavors to find the secret of life end in frustration. Pleasure does not last; work does not satisfy; fame is whimsical; knowledge is incomplete; and life is short. Everything that happens seems predetermined by God, but we cannot understand why it happens.

3. The Advice About Life (2:24-26; 5:1-7; 7:1–8:9; 8:15–12:8). Since life is basically meaningless and empty, the highest good lies in admitting this openly and in enjoying the few fleeting pleasures while one is able (9:7-9). If one waits too long, one may not be physically capable of enjoying these things (11:9–12:8). Yet unbridled living is bad, so live in moderation (7:1-7, 11-22; 8:1-9) and cautiousness (7:8-10; 11:1-8), remembering that people cannot be trusted too much (7:23-29).

The book concludes with the additonal note that the aim of the author has been to teach others so that they will not make the same mistakes as the author. The final verses with their admonition to fear and obey God (12:13-14) are probably a later addition. But it is possible that they may simply be a reflection of a fatalistic, cheerless recognition of the sovereignty of God.

Why is the book in the canon? Perhaps it is because it can remind us that from the human perspective alone life does appear this way—with no purpose, no destiny, and no goal. Thus, by contrast, the significance of revelation and our own encounter with God can be shown to us. As Job finally proclaimed, God is always ultimately mysterious, but yet is also always sovereign love and care.

- How does an understanding of the nature of wisdom literature help us to interpret the various verses of Proverbs 3:1-10? Do we have a right to expect such rewards today? How would these rewards be evidenced?
- Is suffering ever caused by sin, as the three friends of Job contended? Can we learn from suffering, as Elihu said? What kinds of tragic or suffering situations in life move beyond the answers of the friends and demand the Lord's answer?
- In what ways does the book of Ecclesiastes mirror our own experiences? What are the values and limitations of its advice?

Additional Resources

Habel, Norman C. *The Book of Job: A Commentary.* Philadelphia: Westminster Press, 1985.

Kidner, F. Derek. *The Proverbs.* Old Testament Commentary Series. Downers Grove, Ill.: Inter-Varsity Press, 1964.

Pope, Marvin H. *Job.* Rev. ed. The Anchor Bible, vol. 15. Garden City, N.Y.: Doubleday, 1965.

Scott, R. B. Y. *Proverbs and Ecclesiastes.* The Anchor Bible, vol. 18. Garden City, N.Y.: Doubleday, 1965.

Whybray, R. N. *Ecclesiastes.* New Century Bible Commentary. Grand Rapids: William B. Eerdmans, 1989.

7

THE PREEXILIC PROPHETS (EIGHTH CENTURY B.C.)

Amos, Hosea, Isaiah 1–39, Micah

Throughout the world of the Old Testament, from Mesopotamia to Egypt, there were prophets, that is, men and women who were aware of having been set apart by deity to proclaim messages or perform certain actions that represented the divine will. So the existence of prophets in Israel was not a unique phenomenon. As with so many other offices (king, priest, wise man) and practices (worship, social legislation, military activity), the prophets in Israel were similar in form to those in surrounding cultures. The uniqueness of the Old Testament prophets, therefore, lies in the content of their message.

INTRODUCTION TO PROPHECY

By the time of the eighth century B.C., prophecy had begun to change from what it had been during the days of Elijah and Elisha. It still had many formal roots with the past. Revelation was received by visions and dreams (Isaiah 1:1; Amos 1:1; 7:1–9:4); and dramatic behavior was often seen (Jeremiah 19; 27–28; 51:59-64; Ezekial 4; 12:17-20). But now prophets were no longer classified as *nabhi,* "one called" as a spokesperson, and *roeh,* "one who sees" hidden things. They were, rather, distinguished by the emphases of their prophecy. On the one hand, there were the "nationalistic" prophets, who were characterized by their belief that Israel could never be destroyed. They held that since the temple sacrifices were being performed and the Lord had made a covenant with Israel, the future of the nation was secure (Jeremiah 7:4; 14:13;

23:9-22). These are often called "false" prophets. On the other hand, there were the "individualistic" prophets, who took no naive view of Israel's future. The country was doomed. Sometimes they saw immediate respite from destruction if the people as a whole repented, but most of the time they viewed the nation as having reached the point of no return (Amos 3:2; Jeremiah 27–28). These latter people, the "true" prophets, were those who gave us the books that bear their names. We shall see, however, that even a "true" prophet could sometimes be a "false" spokesperson for the Lord.

1. The Composition of Prophecy. Our knowledge of prophetic activity has come to us in two ways, distinguished by the names "Former Prophets" and "Latter Prophets." The names do not so much refer to their time of composition as to their place in the canon and to the fact that they contain two kinds of prophetic materials. We have already seen that the Former Prophets (Joshua, Judges, Samuel, Kings) contain discussions of prophetic ministry within the context of historical reports. These are the result of the historian's art in telling the story of God's activity in history. The Latter Prophets (Isaiah, Jeremiah, Ezekiel, the Twelve "Minor" Prophets), however, are not histories, but they are collections of the prophets' words, along with biographical and autobiographical narratives. Thus, they are not "books" in the sense of being integrated treatises that show a logical progression of thought. They are collections of materials that have been brought together without serious concern for chronological or logical sequence. Therefore, the prophetic books are hard to outline and read. However, Habakkuk and Nahum appear to be unified liturgies with a central theme, and Isaiah 40–55 (usually called Second Isaiah) is a theological treatise composed as a unit.

The process of composition involved both the prophet and the prophet's disciples. The prophet would deliver a message orally and publicly, and those words would be remembered and passed on orally by the prophet's disciples. Scholars have shown us how the ability to memorize was highly developed in the ancient world and have demonstrated that oral transmission played a part in the preservation of literature. There is a great deal of discussion, however, about just how much of a role oral transmission had and when the materials were committed to writing. What is clear, and what is important for our purposes here, is that both written and oral transmission were used. Sometimes the prophet may have written down the actual message; at least, we have evidence in Jeremiah 36 that Jeremiah dictated his words to his scribe Baruch. Isaiah 8:16 indicates that when Isaiah's words were rejected by the people, he had them preserved among his disciples, most likely by writing. But the present books, for the most part, are probably not the work of the prophets themselves any more than the Gospels were written by Jesus himself. The remembered preaching of the prophets has been combined with incidents in the life of each as remembered by unknown prophetic disciples. These materials do not reflect all that each prophet said or did; rather, they reflect only those things that expressed the basic character of the ministry.

The collection of the prophetic materials was usually made on two bases. *First,* in general the editors usually grouped materials together around common themes. So the Book of Jeremiah is arranged as follows: doom oracles against Judah (Jeremiah 2:1–25:13), salvation oracles regarding Israel and Judah (Jeremiah 26–35), selected accounts of events in Judah (Jeremiah 26–35), selected accounts of events in Jeremiah's life (Jeremiah 36–45), doom oracles against the nations (Jeremiah 46–51), and an historical appendix (Jeremiah 52). The materials that formed these large groupings came from different periods in the prophet's life, but they have been arranged thematically, not chronologically. Notice the nonchronological arrangement indicated by Jeremiah 21:1; 24:1; 25:1; 26:1; 27:1; and 28:1. *Second,* within the large groupings, material was often collected on the basis of "catchwords." In other words, two separate prophetic messages contained some common words, and these became the key by which they were remembered together. For example, Jeremiah 3:1–4:2 contains a series of brief sayings (3:1-5; 3:6-10; 3:11-13; 3:14–4:2) each of which contains the catchword "return." Isaiah 1:4-9 is a separate prophetic saying from 1:10-20, but they have been linked together by the catchwords "Sodom" and "Gomorrah" in 1:9 and 1:10.

All of this, of course, warns us that we cannot read the prophetic books as sustained essays, but we should read them as anthologies. A translation that attempts to separate the various parts of the books can be helpful.

2. The Forms of Prophecy. The prophetic books are rich in a variety of literary forms. Virtually the whole range of types of literature was utilized by the prophets and their disciples. Overall, however, as Claus Westermann has helped us to see, there are in the prophetic books three basic speech forms.[7]

a. *Reports.* These are the biographical and autobiographical narratives about the prophets and their experiences. This form is similar to the prose material we saw in the books of Samuel and Kings. Some of the Latter Prophets do not contain any of this type (for example Micah, Habakkuk, Zephaniah), some very little (Amos 7:10-17), but others have a great deal (Jeremiah, Ezekiel, Jonah).

b. *Words directed from God.* This is the material that comprises the prophets' public proclamations, and such material is usually in poetic form (but not always; see Jeremiah 7:1-15). Since it is intended to be God's word that is being transmitted by God's spokesperson, it is often introduced by some formula that contains the name of the Lord. The most common formula is "Thus says the LORD" (Amos 2:1), but this can vary in many ways ("Thus the LORD showed me," "The LORD said," and so forth), and sometimes the formula occurs at the end of a message (for example, Jeremiah 3:13). Because these are messages from the Lord, it must be remembered that the personal pronoun "I" refers to God, even though the message is being delivered by the prophet. So the prophet, in the name of the Lord, rebukes, threatens, commands, promises, and so on.

c. *Words directed to God.* These are in the form of prayers or psalms, again usually in poetry. Often they are reactions to a contemporary situation of the kind described in the reports. Here the "I" refers to the prophet, not the Lord. It is not known whether these were delivered publicly or not. Thus Jeremiah utters his cry in Jeremiah 8:18–9:9, or Habakkuk prays in chapter 3.

It is important to remember that the prophets were preachers who often delivered their words in emotion-charged situations. Since their messages many times condemned public morals or contradicted national hopes, most of these prophets were unpopular. As a result they had to speak quickly and in a compelling fashion. Jonah's words: "Yet forty days and Nineveh shall be overthrown" (Jonah 3:4) are typical. The prophets would have given greater explanation when pressed, but apparently this was not usually the case. So it is understandable that given such situations for preaching, the prophets often used vivid imagery and exaggeration. Through Zephaniah, Yahweh threatens to sweep everything from the face of the earth (Zephaniah 1:2), although a later qualification says that a righteous remnant will be left (2:3). Isaiah promises that "the streams of Edom shall be turned to pitch" (34:9) and that Mount Zion shall become the highest mountain in the world (2:2). Amos looks forward to the day when "the mountains shall drip sweet wine" (9:13). Consequently, the reader of the prophetic literature must always be conscious of this style, lest the prophet be taken too literally. Isaiah had promised the Babylonian exiles that when they returned to Palestine, the "desert shall rejoice and blossom; like the crocus it shall blossom abundantly, and rejoice with joy and singing" (Isaiah 35:1-2). There was no fertile desert at the time of the exiles' return, and Isaiah knew there would not be. He was speaking hyperbolically of the joy that would come to the world at the release of the captives. To miss this point and to point to the future for its fulfillment (as some Bible teachers have done) is to miss the beauty of the prophetic imagery.

3. The Emphases of Prophecy. The prophets were people of their times, and their message was concerned with the specific problems of their own day. They were not theologians propounding doctrine, although this task is important. They were preachers who sought to judge their contemporary life in all of its aspects and to see if it measured up to Yahweh's standard. They addressed their words to the people in Judah and Israel, to the leadership of those people, and to other nations. So even when they spoke of the future, as they did on occasion, their purpose was not to chart the course of events for later generations but to show how present behavior had certain consequences and how Yahweh's will was being worked out in history.

In the process of their preaching, the prophets stressed three things. *First,* they emphasized that only by dependence on God as the source and guide for life can there come stability and security for a people. Since Yahweh was the sovereign Lord of history, then loyalty to Yahweh's pattern of life was the way to life. This message was directed not only to the Israelites but also to other nations. The only difference was that the message was spelled out in different terms. To Israel the message was to return to covenant obligations (Hosea 6:1-11; Amos 2:4 and following verses). To other nations it was a message to return to basic human obligations (Amos 1:3–2:3). *Second,* the prophets stressed that there was an urgency about one's decision regarding God. They felt that the world was in tremendous uproar over the evils of humankind (Jeremiah 2:12-13). Disaster was at hand. Sometimes the prophets thought that destruction could be delayed if positive action was taken immediately (Amos 5:4-7, 14-15), but at other times, they saw the end as inevitable (Amos 8:2-3; Zephaniah 1:7). Too long had people been unconcerned about the evils that surrounded them. *Third,* there was a concern among the prophets to point out that religion and social concern could not be separated. Only by a demonstration of morality and righteousness in all areas of life—moral government, social justice, personal uprightness—could a people expect to have a secure future. Unless basic human needs were cared for, then even the most glorious worship was an abomination to the Lord (Isaiah 1:10-21; Jeremiah 7:1-15).

THE BOOK OF AMOS

The great individual prophets began to arrive on the scene during the deceptive political period of the middle eighth century B.C. On the surface things looked good. The divided kingdoms of Israel and Judah were both recovering from a period of recession. Prosperity and stability were the hallmarks of life. But beneath the surface of official life, off in the corners of the nations, things were bad. Prosperity was being built on oppression, graft, social inequality, and political machinations. So the great prophets were called to go to the northern and southern kingdoms and to point the people to the realities of their lives. They faced an unpopular and immensely difficult job, namely, to speak largely of gloom, to condemn, and to warn in a situation where people wanted to rejoice. The prophets came, therefore, as persons of crisis in times when the majority wanted to believe there was no crisis as serious as that prophesied by the prophets. We call this the "preexilic" period and date it from the arrival of the first of the prophets (Amos) around 750 B.C. through the downfall of the northern kingdom of Israel in 721 B.C. to the destruction of Judah in 597–587 B.C. The common concern of all of these prophets is the political upheaval that eventually engulfed both kingdoms.

1. The Historical Setting. Amos moved into the northern kingdom of Israel from his home in southern Judah when Israel was at the apogee of its power and luxury under Jeroboam II. The time was around 750 B.C. The way for this prosperity had been laid in 803 B.C. by the Assyrian ruler Adad-nirari III when he had conquered Damascus. Now Israel and Judah were free to dominate the trade routes through and around Palestine. Under the agressive leadership of Jeroboam II, the Israelites were able to extend the boundaries of their kingdom, and so the king became known as the savior of his country (2 Kings 13:4-5; 14:25-27). Expensive goods poured into Samaria, the capital city. Fine buildings were erected; physical abundance was common; and the religious system of feasts and sacrifices was humming. But hand in hand with prosperity went oppression, immorality, and injustice. Merchants, urged on by their rapacious wives (Amos 4:1), sought to satisfy their greed by devious means. Mortgages were foreclosed for the smallest debt (2:6); judges were bribed to secure the desired verdict (6:12); weights and measures were falsified (8:5); and bad wheat was sold for good (8:6). Although sacrifices were abundant, they were invalidated by the lives of the worshipers (5:21-24). So Amos prophesied to a country of great contrasts—abundant wealth for a few and abysmal poverty for many. The rich got richer and the poor poorer, and Amos directed the burden of his words to the wealthy leadership. "Beneath the fair surface of prosperity he could detect the rotting mass of spiritual corruption . . . and he knew that, without righteousness, fair dealing, truthfulness, and a recognition of the status of humanity, the nation was doomed."[8]

2. The Prophet. Not much is known about Amos, the man. He was a shepherd (1:1; 7:14) from the town of Tekoa, about ten miles south of Jerusalem. He was also a fruit farmer (7:14), for a "dresser of sycamore trees" was one who cared for the small, fig-like fruit produced by the tree. Whether or not Amos owned his flocks and orchards is not known, but the fact that he "followed" the flock and "dressed" the trees may suggest that he was only a hired employee. The important fact for us, however, is that Amos left his usual occupation to speak as a prophet or spokesman for the Lord in another country. This is the import of his words in 7:14-15.

3. The Message. Various groups of material have been deliberately structured to lead to a logical climax. Whether this is the work of Amos himself or of a group of his disciples is not clear. After the superscription (1:1) has set the time and place, the book begins with a verse that summarizes the theme of Amos's ministry (1:2). He brings a twofold message of imminent danger ("The LORD roars") and severe destruction ("the top of Carmel withers"). As a lion roars when it springs on its victim, so the Lord is in the process of leaping on the prey, Israel. The destruction that will result will mean the devastation of even the lushest part of the country.

Amos's *first* major emphasis is on the sovereignty of Yahweh over all people and all nations (1:3–2:16). Every nation is responsible to Yahweh, since there are no other gods. The terms of that obligation may vary from group to group, but each is subject to God's will. Amos presents this teaching in dramatic fashion. In a series of brief oracles, each introduced by the same formula, the prophet enumerates the sins of the neighboring nations (1:3–2:5). Then as a climax he denounces the people in northern Israel to whom he has been sent (2:6-16). Every nation is guilty of "rebellion" against Yahweh; this is a better translation of the word that recurs throughout this section and which is usually rendered "transgression." But the terms of that rebellion are spelled out differently. For the nations outside Judah and Israel, the sin is in reference to social and humanitarian behavior common to all cultures—cruelty, slave trading, truce breaking, barbarity, and insult. For the convenant nations the indictment concerns social and religious behavior that was specifically spelled out in the Law. Behavior is judged on the basis of the nation's ability to be held responsible, but all people are Yahweh's concern.

In the *second* collection of material, Amos concentrates on the problems of Israel (3:1–6:14). Here he sets the dominant note at the very start (3:1-2). Recalling the exodus from Egypt as a reminder to the people that they had been elected by Yahweh and had entered into a covenant, the prophet then utters the trenchant words: "You only have I known of all the families of the earth; therefore I will punish you for all your iniquities." All nations are responsible to Yahweh, but Israel has a special obligation because of its close relationship with God. The greater the privilege, the greater the responsibility. Yet Amos is intent on pointing out, all through this section, that Israel had not accepted this obligation. Israel thought that this relationship was a matter of inherited privilege sustained by making certain that sacrifices were offered but not by worrying about the will of Yahweh in everyday affairs for justice and morality. This is epitomized in 5:4-5, 14-15, 21-24. But since loyalty to Yahweh involved all of life and since Israel had not responded in this regard, judgment was coming. This comes out particularly in his words about the "day of the LORD" (5:18-20). The origin of the phrase is unknown; perhaps it is related to the idea of Yahweh's military victory. We use the phrase somewhat the same way when we speak of people having "their day." In any case, in the popular mind the "day" would be the time when God would destroy the enemies of Israel and when the nation would experience worldwide domination and prosperity. But Amos and later other prophets brought this interpretation to a violent halt. The "day" would be darkness and violence for the nation.

The *third* emphasis is found in a collection of visions, oracles, and a report (7:1–9:10). Here, too, Amos deals specifically with Israel, and his purpose is to sound a note of irrevocable judgment. At the center of this collection are the five visions that show a progression in God's dealings with Israel leading to judgment. The prophet intends to stress that Israel has reached the point of no return; judgment is inevitable. The turning point comes with the third vision. The first two visions (7:1-3, 4-6) depict natural disasters, commonly the cause of national lamentation—locust plague and drought. These are meant to be typical examples of God's warnings (see 4:6-13). Each time the disaster is averted by the intercession of Amos. But with the third vision (7:7-9), there comes a change: "I will never again pass by them" (7:8; see 8:2; 9:1). Now judgment is irrevocable, and intercession is not allowed. The final two visions (8:1-3; 9:1-6) confirm and repeat this emphasis.

The book concludes with a *fourth* section (9:11-15). Here is the prophet's note of hope. Some feel that this is a later addition, since the rest of the book is characterized by doom. Yet this is to deny to Amos any understanding beyond the immediate situation. The fact that he can talk elsewhere about repentence (5:4, 14), and sees Yahweh as a universal God who will not utterly destroy Israel (9:7-8), makes it plausible that Amos gave us these final words. Here he simply says that the end of Israel politically was not the end of Israel as God's servant. Amos 9:11-12 is quoted in Acts 15:16-17 as fulfilled in the establishment of the church.

THE BOOK OF HOSEA

There was one other prophet to the northern kingdom of Israel during this period—Hosea. All of the rest of the prophets ministered in the south, in Judah. In contrast to Amos, Hosea was a citizen of the north and reflects in his prophecy more compassion and sympathy for Israel.

1. The Historical Setting. Hosea may have been a contemporary with Amos, but probably he began his ministry at the close of Amos's days, after 750 B.C. Hosea 1:1 dates the time span of his work not only during the reign of Uzziah (as does Amos) but also during the reigns of Jotham, Ahaz, and Hezekiah, kings of Judah. This would carry the prophet down to at least 715 B.C., when Hezekiah ascended the throne in the south. When Hosea began, the tone of the national situation was different than that in the time of Amos. Where in Amos the mood is of unconcerned luxury and relative stability, in Hosea there are references to political crises and social disturbances (4:1-3; 7:1-13; 8:4). The old order is breaking up. The prosperity of Jeroboam's early days is being threatened. This would fit the desperate days of the third quarter of the eighth century when the Assyrian armies were on the move, when Israelite kings were assassinated, and when there was political panic. Thus, Hosea apparently began his ministry in the last days of Jeroboam (786–746 B.C.), since 1:4 mentions that his dynasty was still standing ("the house of Jehu"). So into these very unsettled times moved the prophet with his divine commentary on the situation. There was still the same corrupt society as faced by Amos, but now it was a thoroughly frightened one.

2. The Prophet. The prophet has not left us much information about himself. We are told that his father's name was Beeri (1:1). In chapters 1 and 3 we also learn the names of his wife and children, as well as the fact that he had a troubled marriage. But anything else has to be inferred from the style and content of his words. His strong compassion and tenderness come out in the description of his relations with his wife (chapters 1–3) and in his stress on Yahweh's love for his people (see 11:1-4, 8). His great literary ability and political insight suggest a background of training in the wisdom schools and of life among the leadership of the nation.

3. The Message. The description of the *marriage of Hosea* (chapters 1–3) presents the first aspect of Hosea's message. This is intended to be symbolic of the relationship between Yahweh and Israel: how it began, what happened to it, and what its future will be. It has had a variety of interpretations, however, since the details are not clear. One problem concerns the historicity of the marriage. Was it a real event, or is it simply an allegory? The latter view seems improbable, since we know that the prophets often engaged in symbolic behavior, and also there is nothing in the book that really suggests we are not to take it at face value. But the real problem concerns the relationship between chapters 1 and 3. Chapter 1 is a third-person report of Hosea's marriage to an adulterous woman named Gomer and of their children who are given symbolic names "Jezreel" (God will scatter/sow), "Lo-ruhämah" (not pitied), and "Lo-ammi" (not my people). But chapter 3 is a first-person report of Hosea's marriage "again" (3:1) to an adultress. In between is a poem interpreting the marriage in terms of judgment upon Israel for its worship of Baal. Consequently, there are many questions. Are chapters 1 and 3 parallel accounts of the same event, or is chapter 3 the sequel of chapter 1? Is the "woman" of 3:1 the same as "Gomer" of 1:3? What kind of woman was

Gomer when Hosea married her? Was she a temple prostitute? Was she immoral before he married her, or did she become unfaithful only after the marriage?

It seems best to conclude that chapters 1–3 describe one basic series of events in Hosea's life intended to symbolize the history of Yahweh with the people of Israel. The story would be this: Hosea married Gomer without knowing of her immorality, but later he discovered that she was unfaithful (1:2-9). Her continued unfaithfulness caused Hosea to divorce her (2:2), and she fell into degradation. But Hosea continued to love Gomer, and so later he sought her out and remarried her (3:1-5). Thus, Hosea's marriage to Gomer, her unfaithfulness, his continuing love, and his restoration of her depict Yahweh's relationship with Israel. To see two different women in chapters 1 and 3 would destroy the meaning of Hosea's message regarding Yahweh's dealings with one nation, Israel. It is a picture of Yahweh's establishment of a covenant with Israel, of Israel's subsequent pagan worship in Canaan, of Israel's future return to Yahweh (notice 2:7), and of Israel's promised blessings. Although this is the general movement in these three chapters, yet the prophet or his disciples have also included a note of promise in 1:10-11 and 2:14-23. This has been done particularly by a play on the names of the children. Originally they symbolized punishment (God will scatter, Israel will not be shown pity, and Israel is not God's people), but in the future they will depict restoration (God will sow, Israel will be shown pity, and Israel will be again God's people).

The bulk of the book describing the *character of Israel* (chapters 4–14) is really an extended commentary on the events of Israel's history. It contains a large collection of individual oracles, mostly brief, without any clear arrangement. The dominant emphasis is on the corrupt condition of Israel, particularly its religion and politics. The section begins with a summary of Israel's condition (4:1-3). The immorality, depravity, and political insecurity of Israel's present life (4:2-3) are due to the fact that "there is no faithfulness or kindness, and no knowledge of God in the land" (4:1). The verse may perhaps be better translated "there is no faithfulness or kindness, that is, no knowledge of God in the land." "Faithfulness" means honesty, fidelity, trustworthiness. "Kindness," a special word in Hebrew, difficult to translate, combines the ideas of love, kindness, and loyalty. It is a common word used to describe the covenant relationship between Yahweh and Israel, but it is also used for human relationships. The lack of both of these can be traced to Israel's failure to "know" the Lord. This key to the book is stated clearly in 4:6: "My people are destroyed for lack of knowledge." What does Hosea mean by "knowledge" of God? He means information about God (2:8), obedient response to God (6:6), and fellowship with God (2:20).

THE BOOK OF ISAIAH (CHAPTERS 1–39)

The Book of Isaiah evidences most clearly the fact that prophetic literature is largely of a compilatory nature. Although we now have one book called *Isaiah,* it really comprises three large collections from widely separated periods of time. Chapters 1–39 come from the preexilic period (eighth century B.C.); chapters 40–55 are from the time of the exile (sixth century B.C.); and chapters 56–66 derive from the postexilic situation (sixth–fifth centuries B.C.). The evidence for this is mainly the historical allusions in the various sections. These three sections usually go by the names: First, Second, and Third Isaiah. This is not because there were three prophets by the name of Isaiah (although this is not impossible), but because these names identify the respective parts of the book. There was one historical prophet called Isaiah from the eighth century, and to the collection of his work, later materials have been added to a larger degree than in any other prophetic book. The reasons for this are unknown, although there is a common eschatological theme that runs through the three sections. Perhaps then, these collections were combined in later days because they traced the development in Israel's history of this common theme.

All of this is important to know, therefore, if one is to read the book correctly. The Book of Isaiah has material from three different periods of time, and much of what is said will take on meaning only by understanding the particular setting from which it comes. Traditionally it was believed that Isaiah wrote all sixty-six chapters. Scholarship has shown us differently. But actually the question of authorship is relatively unimportant. Crucial to interpretation is recognizing the historical setting of the various parts. So discussion of Second and Third Isaiah will be reserved until later.

1. The Historical Setting. Isaiah's ministry began, on his own reckoning (6:1), in the year King Uzziah of Judah died. This was around 742 B.C. Thus, Isaiah was basically the southern counterpart of Hosea, who had begun his work a few years earlier. The times were politically troubled in both Israel and Judah. Uzziah had been a good king (783–742 B.C.). He had brought great prosperity to the country of Judah and had encouraged the worship of Yahweh, but he had not gone far enough in building a stable social life. There was too wide a gap between rich and poor, too much injustice and oppression. His prosperous reign was made possible because there were no foreign powers at this time who tried to test the stability of the nation. Toward the end of his rule, Assyria began to look outside its boundaries for territories to conquer, and from this time onward Judah's political fortunes began to decline. Uzziah's successors continued to protect the indulgence of the rich at the expense of the poor, sought to delude the people into a sense of security because the temple sacrifices were being offered, and tried to stave off the armies of Assyria by a series of political maneuvers. From 735 B.C. onward Judah became a vassal of Assyria, and although it tried revolt on various occasions, Judah never again was an independent state, except for a brief period in the second century B.C. Isaiah attempted to minister to Jerusalem during these days of declining glory from 742–701 B.C. We last heard of him when he counseled Hezekiah to resist an Assyrian onslaught on Jerusalem in 701 B.C., and he promised that it would not be taken at that time (29:5-8; 37:33-35). The city remained as Isaiah had said, but after this he was heard of no more.

Reading the Book of Isaiah is not easy, since the contents are not arranged chronologically, nor do they clearly identify the political and social situations to which they were addressed. Yet if we are to catch the point of the prophetic word, much depends on understanding the historical background. It appears that there are three specific periods during Isaiah's forty-year ministry from which we have had material preserved. Although it is not always certain which passage belongs in which period, the reader should keep these three periods in mind.

The *first* period of Isaiah's ministry covered the years 742–734 B.C., that is, between the death of King Uzziah and the war with Syria and Israel. During most of these days, Judah was enjoying economic prosperity and political success, and much of Isaiah's work was concerned with denouncing social and religious evils (1–5). Toward the end of this time Assyrian armies were advancing towards Palestine; and Syria and Israel sought to get Judah to join with them to resist the advance (2 Kings 16). Isaiah was against this and also against King Ahaz' decision to join forces with the Assyrians (7–8; 9:8-21; 17:1-6; 28:1-4). He knew that allegiance to Assyria meant allegiance to Assyria's gods, since tribute and the erection of pagan altars would be the price of protection (2 Kings 16:10-16). But Isaiah's counsel was rejected, and the prophet appears to have withdrawn from public life to a teaching ministry among his disciples (8:16-18). During his conversations with Ahaz, Isaiah gave the famous promise of the birth of a child to be called Immanuel (literally, "God with us"), who would be a sign of Yahweh's protecting presence with Judah (7:10-17). The immediate reference of the sign was to a contemporary child known to both the king and the prophet, since the Hebrew text may be translated to read: "Behold, the young woman has conceived and is about to bear a son" (7:14, author's translation). But the promise was used by Matthew (1:23) as an analogy for the birth of Jesus Christ, another "sign" of the presence of God.

The *second* period of Isaiah's public work (716–711 B.C.) did not begin until a new king, Hezekiah, had ascended to the throne in Judah in 716 B.C. Isaiah expressed great expectations for his reign with two promises that embody the ancient conception of the king as a mediator of divine blessings (9:2-7; 11:1-9). This close relationship with God comes out clearly in the gift of the "Spirit" in chapter 11 and in the titles given to the king, which are perhaps more clearly translated: "a wonder of a counselor, a god of a warrior, a father of perpetuity, a prince of peace" (9:6). Hezekiah started in grand fashion, instituting a reform (2 Kings 18:3-6), but early in his reign he was pressured by Egypt and Philistia to revolt against Assyria. Isaiah opposed this; and apparently Hezekiah listened to him, for when the Assyrians crushed the rebellion in 711 B.C., Judah was spared. Isaiah's words during this time are found scattered throughout the book (14:28-32; 18; 20; 22:1-11; 28:1-22; 29:1-24; 30:1-17; 31:1-3).

The *third* period falls between 705 and 701 B.C. Again a political event claimed Isaiah's attention. In 705 B.C., after the death of Sargon II, king of Assyria, a general revolt broke out among the vassal nations. This time Hezekiah took an active part (2 Kings 18:7ff.; 19:1-37). The revolt ultimately failed when Sargon's successor, Sennacherib, devastated the country in 701 B.C., even though he was not able to capture Jerusalem (Isaiah 1:4-9; 10:5-16, 24-32; 14:24-27; scattered passages in 28–32; 36–39). During this period Isaiah sought to show that the coming of the Assyrians was the judgment of God and that, nevertheless, Jerusalem would be spared and the Assyrians ultimately punished. This interpretation is epitomized in 10:5-15.

2. The Prophet. Isaiah, as with all of the prophets, remains somewhat hidden behind his message. He was the son of Amoz (1:1; not to be confused with the prophet Amos), and all of his recorded prophecies seem to suggest that he lived his whole life in Jerusalem. He tells us that he was married to a "prophetess" (8:3) and that he had two sons to whom he gave symbolic names (7:3; 8:3). Much more than this we do not know. Some have suggested that Isaiah came from an aristocratic and influential family, since he could approach the king with ease (7:3) and had friends among the leadership (8:2). But this is not compelling evidence, so we do not know for sure. His life shows the great courage that was typical of the prophets, and his message illustrates the graphic, bold imagery so often found in their preaching. Isaiah even called the inhabitants of Jerusalem "harlots" (1:21), not the kind of language designed to ease tensions. The date of his death is uncertain, although a Jewish legend in a book called *The Ascension of Isaiah* (first century A.D.) claims he was killed in the reign of Manasseh (687–642 B.C.).

3. The Message. Isaiah was primarily a man of the political scene. His concern was with the intrigues of international politics and with the social and religious practices in Judah that made these intrigues necessary. He approached these political problems with the dominant conception, gained at his call, of the sovereign holiness of Yahweh and of Yahweh's involvement in the world. Isaiah was a prophet of the "present" and of God's work in the present. Characteristic in his description of Yahweh is the phrase "the Holy One of Israel" (1:4; 5:19, 24; 10:17, 20; 30:11, 15; 31:1; see 6:3). By this he was emphasizing the awesome lordship of God over people and nations, a lordship that would not allow evil to continue unpunished. Throughout Isaiah's oracles appear two primary conceptions. *First,* the prophet denounces the "pride" of humans that causes them to think they can live independently of God. Humans' sin is their failure to recognize and believe in God (2:6ff.; 3:16ff.; 9:8ff.; 10:5ff.; 22:15ff.; 28:1ff.). This idea is found in all areas of Judah's life. This pride led to unwise political alliances and to dependence upon armament, and thus it brought about Judah's destruction (3:9; 30:1-2; 31:1-3). *Second,* Isaiah proclaims the need for "trust" in Yahweh. Those who accept their dependence on God will have a future because God is the one who is guiding history. This is epitomized in 26:3: "Thou dost keep him in perfect peace, whose mind is stayed on thee, because he trusts in thee" (see 7:3, 9; 28:16; 30:15). There was a realism in Isaiah's words. Judah did not have the geographical or economic ability to play power politics. Its importance lay in its role as a "kingdom of priests" (Exodus 19:6), and its security lay in political neutrality. It was this thinking that was behind Isaiah's counsel of trust in Yahweh.

THE BOOK OF MICAH

1. The Historical Setting. The last of the eighth century B.C. prophets, Micah, labored for some time alongside Isaiah in the capital city of Jerusalem. They did not begin together, for Isaiah preceded Micah by a few years. Isaiah began at the death of Uzziah (742 B.C.), but Micah dates his ministry in the days of Jotham, Ahaz, and Hezekiah (1:1), that is, between 735 and 687 B.C. at the longest. The prophet's actual labors, however, were probably somewhat shorter. The problem is that Micah speaks so generally of conditions in the political arena that it is difficult to know dates for sure. All we can say is that he moved about Jerusalem during the frantic days of Assyria's mounting influence in Palestine. The threat of imminent destruction of Samaria in the north (1:2-9) and the claim of Jeremiah that Micah was active during Hezekiah's reign (Jeremiah 26:17-18) suggest a date between 725 and 701 B.C. For details of this period, see the previous section on Isaiah.

2. The Prophet. Micah was of country origin; perhaps he was a farmer. We are informed (1:1, 14) that he came from Moresheth-gath, a small village in the hill country of Judah, southwest of Jerusalem on the border with Philistia. Apparently, like Amos, he was not a professional prophet, but under the impetus of the Spirit of the Lord (3:8), Micah strode out of the hills to denounce the oppression, the injustice, the idolatry, and the naive optimism of the people of Judah. No one escaped his scathing tongue; in particular, he leveled his blasts against the leadership in Jerusalem—the rich, the rulers, the priests, and the prophets (2:1-5, 8-9; 3:1-5, 9-11). Here Micah betrays something of his country background, as he denounces the oppression of the small farmer by the wealthy (2:1-5) and speaks agonizingly of the destructive results on the towns of southern Judah caused by the corruption of Jerusalem's leadership (1:10-16).

3. The Message. The overall message of the book can perhaps best be grasped by noting the threefold occurrence of the word "hear" (1:2; 3:1; 6:1). These divide the book into three parts, each of which shows the typical arrangement of prophetic material into the double pattern of disaster and deliverance. The *first* (1:2–2:13) begins with a collection of doom oracles directed against Israel and Judah (1:2–2:11), and it concludes with a promise of restoration (2:12-13). This section opens with a brief passage, in the form of a trial scene, that summarizes the message of Micah (1:2-9). This passage begins with an announcement of the trial of Israel and Judah (1:2-4). Here the imminence of judgment is stressed by the words "the LORD is coming." Then it details the divine indictment of the people, concentrating on the root of their injustice and immorality, namely, idolatry (1:5-7). Finally, it includes a lament by the prophet about the coming destruction that will engulf both nations (1:8-9). The *second* part (3:1–5:15) again begins with an announcement of doom (3:1-12). This time it specifically mentions the leaders as the object of his wrath—the rulers, because they "skin" the populace (3:2), the prophets, because they lead them astray (3:5), and the total group, because they allow themselves to be bribed (3:11). This section then concludes with a lengthy series of promises regarding a bright future (4:1–5:15). Here two things are stressed. In chapter 4 the prophet details the messianic kingdom where Jerusalem will be the center of the world and there will be unparalleled peace. Micah 4:1-4 is a quotation, with slight variation, from Isaiah 2:1-4. Chapter 5 next provides a description of the messianic king who will come from Bethlehem, the ancestral home of the Davidic king. The *third* part (6:1–7:20) repeats the pattern of disaster (6:1–7:7) and restoration (7:8-20). Once again there is a courtroom scene at the beginning (6:1-8), containing one of the finest expressions of prophetic theology (6:8): "the justice for which Amos pleaded, the steadfast love *(hesedh)* that is central to the teaching of Hosea, and the humble trust that Isaiah saw as the only fit response of man to the holiness of Yahweh."[9]

- How do the prophets illustrate the important fact that Israel's life and institutions were both similar to and different from the surrounding culture? Where does the uniqueness of the Old Testament therefore lie?
- How were the Israelites able to distinguish between true and false prophets? Could a person be both? Is there a problem today? How can we determine the difference in present-day claims for the will of God?
- In what areas does the prophetic message need application today? Think here of both the personal and social scenes. How can the contemporary church become prophetic?
- What parallels exist between the historical situation of the eighth century B.C. in Palestine and the twentieth century A.D. in our country?
- What are some implications of Amos's view of all humanity's responsibility to God (see Acts 10:35; Romans 2:12-16)? Does this have a bearing on the problem of universalism?
- In what ways can judgment or disaster become irrevocable? What is the difference between forgiveness and escape from trouble?

- What does it mean to "know" God?
- How does Isaiah illustrate the prophetic role in political affairs? What are legitimate and illegitimate roles of the church in political and social matters?
- What is idolatry? In what ways is idolatry present today?

Additional Resources on Prophecy

Anderson, George W. *A Critical Introduction to the Old Testament.* 2nd ed. Naperville, Ill.: Alec R. Allenson, 1960.

Anderson, George W. *The History and Religion of Israel.* New York: Oxford University Press, 1966.

Blenkinsopp, Joseph. *A History of Prophecy in Israel: From the Settlement in the Land to the Hellenistic Period.* Philadelphia: Westminster Press, 1983.

Heschel, Abraham J. *The Prophets.* New York: Harper & Row, 1962.

Koch, Klaus. *The Prophets: The Assyrian Period.* Philadelphia: Fortress Press, 1982.

Additional Resources on Specific Prophets

Andersen, Francis I., and Freedman, David Noel. *Amos.* The Anchor Bible, vol. 24A. Garden City, N.Y.: Doubleday, 1989.

Andersen, Francis I., and Freedman, David Noel. *Hosea.* The Anchor Bible, vol. 24. Garden City, N.Y.: Doubleday, 1980.

Hillers, Delbert R. *Micah.* Philadelphia: Fortress Press, 1983.

Kaiser, Otto. *Isaiah 1–12, A Commentary.* 2nd ed. Philadelphia: Westminster Press, 1983.

Kaiser, Otto. *Isaiah 13–39, A Commentary.* Philadelphia: Westminster Press, 1974.

Mauchline, John. "The Book of Hosea." In *The Interpreter's Bible,* edited by George A. Buttrick et al., vol. 6, 553-725. Nashville: Abingdon Press, 1956.

Mays, James L. *Amos: A Commentary.* Philadelphia: Westminster Press, 1969.

Mays, James L. *Hosea: A Commentary.* Philadelphia: Westminster Press, 1969.

Scott, R. B. Y. "The Book of Isaiah, Chapters 1–39." In *The Interpreter's Bible,* edited by George A. Buttrick et al., vol. 5, 151-381. Nashville: Abingdon Press, 1956.

Wolfe, Rolland E. "The Book of Micah." In *The Interpreter's Bible,* edited by George A. Buttrick et al., vol. 6, 897-949. Nashville: Abingdon Press, 1956.

Wolff, H. W. *Joel and Amos.* Edited by Dean McBride. Translated by Waldemar Janzen. Philadelphia: Fortress Press, 1977.

8

THE PREEXILIC PROPHETS (SEVENTH CENTURY B.C.)

Zephaniah, Habakkuk, Nahum, Jeremiah

There were four preexilic prophets who labored during the seventh century B.C.—Zephaniah, Habakkuk, Nahum, and Jeremiah. Seventy years passed after Micah before a prophetic voice was heard again in Jerusalem that was important enough to be preserved.

THE BOOK OF ZEPHANIAH

1. The Historical Setting. The superscription dates Zephaniah during the reign of Josiah of Judah (640–609 B.C.). Since the prophet condemns the worship of other gods in Jerusalem (1:4-5), the time must be before 621 B.C. when Josiah instituted a great reform that sought to purge the country of idolatry (2 Kings 23). Thus Zephaniah had a brief ministry centering around 630 B.C. This was a time of transition in Judah's life. When Micah last spoke, the country was under the rule of good King Hezekiah, who had managed to maintain a measure of autonomy and religious purity while being a vassal to Assyria. But under Hezekiah's son and successor, Manasseh (687–642 B.C.), the nation began to slip more and more into apostasy and domination by Assyria. Fertility worship reappeared, and pagan altars were erected in the temple (2 Kings 21:1-18). The same situation was maintained under Manasseh's son Amon (642–640 B.C.; 2 Kings 21:20-22). But when Amon was assassinated and eight-year-old Josiah came to power, the way was open to a new day. Assyria had begun to wane as an international force, and thus Judah was left relatively free to pursue its own policies. Into this situation stepped Zephaniah with a vision for what could be if the nation would return to Yahweh, but yet with a realism that knew there was a certain destructive inevitability to the behavior of the people. His relationship to the royal court—he was possibly a relative of King Hezekiah, if this is the meaning of the reference in 1:1—had given Zephaniah peculiar insight into the problems of his nation.

2. The Message. The message of Zephaniah resembles in many respects that of Amos, Hosea, and Micah. *First,* he attacks the idolatry, the imitation of pagan religious rites, and the deceptive self-confidence of the people (1:4-6, 8-9, 12; 3:1-7). In this way he prepared the way for Josiah's reform. Graphically Zephaniah describes the people of Jerusalem as those who no longer took Yahweh seriously as a factor in life (1:12*b*) and who were "thickening upon their lees" (1:12*a*), that is, were indolently content with themselves. *Second,* he therefore rails against them and threatens terrible divine judgment on "the day of the LORD" (1:2-3, 7, 18; 2:1-2). Here he expands the teaching of his predecessors Amos (5:18-20) and Isaiah (2:6-22). Disaster, claims Zephaniah, is going to sweep away humankind, the inhabitants of Judah and of all nations, from the face of the earth. Some have thought that Zephaniah was referring here to a specific invasion from the north by the Scythians, but the prophet nowhere mentions them. *Third,* there is also a message of hope in the midst of gloom, although the latter is the dominant note of the book. If the people would repent, "perhaps" (2:3) the coming judgment would not be so severe for them as it otherwise would be (see 2:8). But, even so, Zephaniah was assured that some would respond, and it would be out of this nucleus, the true remnant, that Yahweh would build the new kingdom (3:9-20). Noteworthy is the promise in 3:9:

> "Yea, at that time I will change
> the speech of the peoples
> to a pure speech,
> that all of them may call on the
> name of the LORD
> and serve him with one accord."
> —Zephaniah 3:9

The future will mean one world serving God when people will be forgiven ("pure speech"; see Isaiah 6:5-7), and the inability to communicate with one another caused by Babel will be reversed (see Genesis 11:1-9). Pentecost and the gift of the Spirit were the beginning of that fulfillment (Acts 2:1-11).

THE BOOK OF HABAKKUK

The Book of Habakkuk deals with one central theme—the destruction of foreign powers. The prophet asks in essence: "Why does Yahweh allow evil people to continue to pursue their oppressive and violent ways?" Yahweh answers: "Trust me." The book therefore presents another form of the common problem of reconciling the existence of evil with the existence of God.

1. The Historical Setting. The historical situation presupposed by the book is not quite clear. Chapter 1:6 gives us the only clue with its mention of the Chaldeans or Babylonians as the agents of God in the destruction of the "wicked" (1:4) which is yet to come. But who are the wicked? Many suggestions have been made, but one of the most common suggestions is that this term refers to evil people in Judah who are so often condemned by the other prophets. Although this is a possible interpretation, perhaps a better approach is, in light of the context, to identify the wicked as the Assyrians, who had followed a policy of ruthless suppression of their enemies, including the people of Judah. Habakkuk plainly refers to a foreign nation as ripe for destruction (2:8) and praises Yahweh for the salvation of the "anointed" (3:13), that is, the king of Judah. Furthermore, the "violence done to Lebanon" (2:17) echoes the statement about the Assyrians in Isaiah 37:24. The Babylonians are already a power known by Habakkuk, and this fact assumes therefore that they had already revolted against the Assyrians (625 B.C.). But since the Assyrians have not yet been destroyed, this would date the book before 612 B.C. Thus Habakkuk is to be dated from the period between 625 and 612 B.C., and the prophet comes from a time of international crisis when the Assyrian power was still oppressive, but when other powers were vying for control. Habakkuk raises the problem of the place of Yahweh and the people of Yahweh in all of this.

2. The Form of the Book. The book does not indict the sins of the people of Judah, but it looks beyond to the destruction of a foreign power. This fact, plus the clear form of the third chapter as a prayer to be sung (notice the musical directions in 3:1, 19), has caused some scholars to identify the book as a prophetic liturgy. The book is not a collection of disparate oracles, but it is a composition intended to be used in temple worship. The unified theme, the dialogue between Yahweh and Habakkuk, the "woe" curses, and the closing prayer all would fit a worship setting better than a marketplace or temple courtyard, particularly since Judah is not directly addressed. If this is so, then Habakkuk was a cult prophet in the service of the Jerusalem temple. He certainly was a professional prophet (1:1).

3. The Message. The central note of the Book of Habakkuk is, of course, found in the words of 2:4: "Behold, he whose soul is not upright in him shall fail, but the righteous shall live by his faith." Unfortunately the Hebrew text of this verse is somewhat obscure, and the first clause is not certain. Probably it should be translated: "Behold, the soul of the proud [literally, the puffed up one] is not secure, but the righteous shall live by his faith." Habakkuk begins by raising the problem of evil (1:2-4). The world in his day is apparently a moral mess. The evil Assyrians are prospering. The response that Habakkuk receives is that God is going to rouse up the Babylonians to destroy them (1:5-11). This only makes the problem worse for Habakkuk—this makes God a partner in evil, since the Babylonians are no better than the Assyrians (1:12–2:1). God's answer is a call to trust in spite of appearances (2:2-5), for wickedness will be destroyed (2:6-20). Thus the book does not solve the problem of evil; it only claims there is a solution in the mind of God. The "proud" person who cannot accept this will therefore crumble spiritually and mentally in the face of evil. The "righteous" person or one who has a trustful "faith" will be able to "live." So Habakkuk's call is to faithfulness. In his view of Yahweh as the Lord of history, even involved in the actions of other nations, Habakkuk has given a basis for this trust. Consequently, the book can conclude with a ringing affirmation about the Lord (3:2-19). In Romans 1:17 and Galatians 3:11, Paul expands the meaning of "live" in Habakkuk 2:4 to designate "eternal life."

THE BOOK OF NAHUM

One theme dominates the Book of Nahum—the destruction of Nineveh, capital of the Assyrian empire. This is similar to the Book of Habakkuk. However, Nahum saw the judgment already taking place, and so he begins with a psalm of praise. Habakkuk wondered when it would take place, and so he started with a psalm of lament.

1. The Historical Setting. Since the destruction of Nineveh is described in breathless tones as a catastrophe near at hand, the book appears to come from around 615 B.C., for Nineveh fell before the armies of the Babylonians and their allies in 612 B.C. This was, therefore, a time of change and uncertainty in Judah. They had long felt the domination of the Assyrians, but now the enemy was gone, or was about to go, and so quite naturally the announcement of Nineveh's demise was expressed with great joy by the prophet. We sense this particularly when we read the savage exultation recorded in 2:3-13.

2. The Prophet. Little is known of Nahum, except the name of his hometown, Elkosh. Its location is unknown, although there have been many guesses. Nahum must have spoken to Judah, since Israel had long since gone as a nation (721 B.C.).

3. The Message. The book is introduced by a fragmentary hymn of praise (1:2-11) reminiscent of the opening of Micah and Zephaniah. Yahweh is depicted as coming with earth-shaking and earth-melting power to sweep away the enemies into the darkness of utter destruction.

The rest of the book is a collection of sayings detailing in poetic imagery the downfall of Nineveh. The sayings seem to be in the form of three successive liturgies (1:12–2:2; 2:3-13; 3:1-7) followed by a mocking song (3:8-17) and a mocking dirge (3:18-19). Notice in the first liturgy the alternation between promise to Judah (1:12, 15; 2:2) and threat to Nineveh (1:14; 2:1). In the second liturgy both Nahum (2:3-12) and Yahweh (2:13) speak in threat against Nineveh. Then in the third, the prophet (3:1-4) and Yahweh (3:5-7) again threaten the capital city. The book concludes first with a song (3:8-17) mocking Nineveh's fall to the enemy, just as

Thebes (3:8), a city in Egypt, fell before the Assyrians (663 B.C.). To this is added a dirge (3:18-19) stressing the finality of the destruction. These liturgical elements have led many scholars to conclude that the book was composed after the downfall of Nineveh to celebrate the event in the Jerusalem temple. Probably it originated as a series of prophetic oracles by Nahum announced at various times in Judah, which were then later gathered together for liturgical use.

The exultation that Nahum expresses in his gleeful look at the details of Nineveh's destruction, including mention of the loss of Assyrian children (3:10), is not unusual among the prophets who lived in those grim days. They were, after all, people of their times. This is how Nahum expressed his understanding of Yahweh as God of history and judge of all people.

THE BOOK OF JEREMIAH

Reading the Book of Jeremiah is, on the one hand, an exercise in frustration, since it is quite a hodgepodge of materials arranged usually without logical or chronological progression. Among the prophetic literature this, of course, is not unique to Jeremiah; it is only that the disarray seems to be most evident in this book. Yet, on the other hand, there is so much detailed information in the book, both about the prophet himself and his times, that the problem of identifying the historical setting is ameliorated on many occasions.

1. The Historical Setting. Perhaps the best way to read the Book of Jeremiah is first to become familiar with the details of the account in 2 Kings 22–25. Jeremiah's career took place in the midst of the events recorded for us in those chapters, and his words are made clearer by keeping them in mind. There we read of the five kings (Josiah, Jehoahaz, Jehoiakim, Jehoiachin, Zedekiah) and one governor (Gedaliah) who ruled Judah during Jeremiah's days. The details of their reigns will not be summarized here, since they are clear for anyone to read in 2 Kings 22–25. However, it will be helpful to notice that Jeremiah's work can be divided into four periods during this time.

The *first* period covers the time from his call (626 B.C.) to the beginning of Josiah's reform (621 B.C.). When Jeremiah began, two important events were in the process of taking place. First, the very year of his call, the Babylonians had broken away from Assyria and were moving to take control of the empire. Second, this political change allowed Josiah freedom to rid the country of the influence of Assyria's idolatrous practices, and so Josiah began a purge. This purge reached a peak in 621 B.C. when workers who were restoring the temple found a copy of the Book of the Law. This became the detailed basis for Josiah's reform. So, with the decline of Assyria, and under the leadership of a strong king, a spirit of nationalism developed in Judah. Most of chapters 1–6 show us the prophet's message during that time and how he reacted. In essence, Jeremiah condemned the corruption of the people in the political, social, and religious realms, accused them of apostasy from the Lord, and announced that an enemy from the north would bring divine judgment on them. In a real sense Jeremiah prepared the way for Josiah's call for reformation in 621 B.C. He was attempting to show that the building of a stable nation in those opportune days would be achieved only by abandoning pagan practices and by returning to Yahweh. This is epitomized by the collection of oracles in 3:1–4:4 that contain the word "return" (3:1, 7, 12, 14, 22; 4:1). Apparently at some time during this period, Jeremiah gave in to a feeling that his preaching was useless, for with ferocious anger he assigns the people to destruction (6:10-11, 27-29).

The *second* period of Jeremiah's ministry is somewhat of a mystery. It extends from Josiah's reform (622 B.C.) to the death of the king (609 B.C.). But nothing in the book can be assigned with any certainty to this time, since our knowledge of the period is scanty. Many scholars feel that after Josiah began his reform, Jeremiah retired from public life for a period that lasted until the death of Josiah in 609 B.C. The reason usually given is that Jeremiah would have been satisfied with the actions of the king and would have had no further need to speak, or else that he became disgusted with the superficiality of the reform and gave up on the people. But this view may be suspect, since the reform was not a real success from the start, and it is doubtful that such a driven person as Jeremiah would have remained quiet. Furthermore, though he longed to run away from it all, he found his call to his people inescapable. So Jeremiah must have taken some action during this period, but it is difficult to assign any passages with clarity. Probably some of the undated passages, which show Jeremiah dissatisfied with the reform and with the continuing injustice, immorality, and false worship, come from this time. He wanted to point out to the people that unless they made their repentence a matter of total life commitment to the covenant obligations, they were due for judgment (see 3:6-10; 8:4-12).

The *third* period is clear, and the bulk of the material in chapters 7–39 has been preserved from this time. It stretches from the death of Josiah (609 B.C.) to the final destruction of the nation (587 B.C.). Josiah's death had been a great shock to the people, for he represented the move towards independence. But he was killed when he resisted an Eygptian army that passed through the country. The Egyptians in turn deposed Josiah's successor, Jehoahaz, and replaced him with a man of their own—Jehoiakim, the brother of Jehoahaz. Now the people began to feel a creeping fear about their future. So they turned to the temple and the round of sacrifices for their security. Pagan worship and practices reappeared. As long as they had the temple, they believed that Yahweh was committed to protect them. It was Jeremiah's task to denounce this false theology and to claim that their continued immorality and injustice would be the cause of the destruction of the temple and the nation (7:1-15; 26:1-24). From this time onward Jeremiah began increasingly to be harassed and persecuted and rejected. Such a response is not too hard to understand. He had wrested from the people of the nation, in their moment of panic, the last security they had. No wonder he was resented and hated. Then after 605 B.C. Jeremiah's preaching brought against him another claim: He was a traitor! In that year Nebuchadnezzar of Babylonia conquered the Egyptians and took control of Palestine. In 597 B.C. his armies captured Jerusalem and put Jehoiakim under vassalage. But then, because Jehoiakim revolted, Nebuchadnezzar returned in 587 B.C. to put down the revolt, to destroy the temple and the city, and to carry away large numbers of captives. During this whole period Jeremiah counseled surrender to the inevitability of Babylonian control (for example, 38:2), which he saw as divine punishment for the sins of Judah (for example, 25). After they had been captured, he asked the people to pray for the welfare of the Babylonian cities (29:7). At the beginning of this period, Jeremiah even dictated a summary of his message during the previous years to Baruch, his scribe (36). Baruch read it publicly in the temple in the hope that the people would repent, even though repentance would not spare them from exile. All of this, of course, was thought to be treasonous preaching. But Jeremiah had a realism about him that is often lacking in days of fervent nationalism and patriotism. His counsel to surrender was based on concern for his people. The Babylonian invasion could not be stopped; resistance would only mean needless shedding of blood. Prayer for Babylonian cities was necessary, since the time was not ripe for subversion. Jeremiah saw, apparently, that the ruthless power of the Babylonians could not last. So throughout this period Jeremiah had to struggle in a lonely, unpopular fight against the leadership and populace of Jerusalem. He barely escaped death many times. He was beaten and thrown into prison (37–38); but after the Babylonians captured the city, they released him (39:11-12).

The *fourth* period is of unknown length, and it extends from the fall of Jerusalem (587 B.C.) to Jeremiah's death in Egypt. It is described in chapters 40–45. The Babylonians put a governor named Gedaliah over Judah, but soon he was assassinated. Since this would inevitably bring reprisals from the Babylonians, a group of Jews fled to Egypt, forcing Jeremiah to accompany them. There he uttered his last words.

2. The Prophet. The prophet had a long ministry that centered primarily in Jerusalem. He received his call in the thirteenth year of Josiah's reign (626 B.C.; 1:2; 25:3), labored through the last forty years of Judah's existence as an independent nation (587 B.C.), and then apparently labored for a few years more in Egyptian exile (43:1-7). He came from a priestly family in the small village of Anathoth, about six miles northeast of Jerusalem (1:1). He was heir to a rich heritage; he preached in immensely important days; yet the record of his life is one of struggle, rejection, and loneliness. His family sought to kill him (12:6); he was accused of treason and threatened by the leadership (20:1-6; 37; 38); he remained unmarried (16:1-2); and his message was, by and large, rejected by the people. Against this background one can understand the vehemence of Jeremiah's words on so many occasions, as well as his wish that he had never been born (15:10) or that he could run away from it all (9:2), or his feeling that God had let him down (20:7). Yet something kept driving him on—the realization that he was proclaiming divine reality—and this "fire in his bones" (20:9) would not let him quit. Because of the dark picture that he often painted about the future of Judah and because of his own personal gloom, Jeremiah has been known through the years as the "weeping prophet." In fact, part of the reason the book of Lamentations has traditionally been attributed to him is because of these things, as well as the statement of 2 Chronicles 35:25 that Jeremiah "uttered a lament" over King Josiah. There is no question that Jeremiah wept, but much of the time he was weeping over his people (8:21).

One of the unique elements of this book is the collection of personal "confessions" scattered throughout the first part of the book. There is no real parallel to these in the other prophetic materials. The confessions are sometimes in the form of a prayer to God, but often they are simply soliloquies. In either case they reflect the reaction of Jeremiah, usually negative, to his personal situation. In this part of the book, we read of Jeremiah's struggle with himself as he is caught in the tension between the call of God and the failure of his work. On occasion the confessions have been preserved for us following one of his oracles of doom (4:19-22) or a biographical narrative (20:7-18). These indicate how the editors interpreted the historical causes for his outbursts. The confessions are found in 4:19-22; 8:18–9:1; 11:18-23; 12:1-6; 15:10, 15-21; 17:14-18; 18:18-23; 20:7-18.

3. The Message. The Book of Jeremiah is fascinating reading both for the intensity of its imagery and for the picture it paints of an earnest, courageous, human servant of God. Jeremiah was no saint in the sense of one who had risen above life's struggles. He was often gloomy both about his country and about the success of his work. He even wondered about God. What was Jeremiah trying to communicate to his contemporaries? He had, of course, the usual task of condemning the moral and social evils of his day. His attacks on the temple and sacrifices were the most severe of all the prophets. He came close to claiming that Yahweh could not care less about sacrifices (6:16-21; 7:21-23). He warned his people about the problems of international politics and constantly spoke of Judah's destruction. Yet he also had a message of hope. Chapters 30–33, often called "The Book of Consolation," promise a future day when Israel and Judah would be reunited and restored in a new kingdom even greater than that of David and Solomon.

Through it all, two dominant notes keep sounding. *First,* there is the absolute conviction that Yahweh is God of all life, involved in the affairs of Judah and Israel, in the history of nations, and in creation itself. Yahweh is Creator (27:5) and Sustainer (31:35-37) of the world, and this assurance is the guarantee that history is not outside of God's control. So God uses Nebuchadnezzar as a "servant" (27:6) in the fulfillment of God's purposes, and those in Judah who have been taken captive by the Babylonian king can still have hope in the future (42:11-12). God can deliver them out of the king's hands. What Jeremiah was attempting to do in proclaiming this message was to provide for his people some ground of faith in the midst of personal and national tragedy. The prophet explained many times that Judah's downfall was just divine retribution for their years of sin; and sin was, in part, selfishly motivated political decisions. The people had assumed that the nation was inviolable because God had chosen it (7:3-4). But Jeremiah showed that even their disaster was part of God's program.

Second, the prophet stresses the individual character of sin and of relationship with Yahweh. Not unaware of the corporate body, Jeremiah lived in a day when the sense of corporate solidarity had deluded the people into thinking that being a member of the people of God was automatically achieved by birth and that the nation would remain secure by an impersonal maintenance of sacrifices. So Jeremiah sought to show that the nation was composed of individuals whose individual decisions and actions affected its future. Each person's heart needed cleansing (4:3-4; 13:23; 17:9), and each person's actions were important (7:5-15; 31:29-30). This comes out clearly in Jeremiah's vision of the future when Yahweh would establish a "new covenant" (31:31-34) by forgiving their sins and changing their hearts so they would respond. Even now, in the present judgment, Yahweh's desire was for the inhabitants of Judah to repent and return, since continuing disaster was not irrevocable (3:1–4:4), and the future was conditional upon response (18:1-12).

- How do we react to the prophets' views of the destruction of the other nations? Can we accept the prophets' intents while rejecting their methods of application?
- In what ways do Jeremiah's "confessions" express anything about our own struggles in faith?
- What are some contemporary illustrations of the effects of the relation between the individual and the group? How far are we really free to make our own decisions? How are we affected by others?

Additional Resources

Bright, John. *Jeremiah.* The Anchor Bible, vol. 21. Garden City, N.Y.: Doubleday, 1965.

Hyatt, J. Philip. *Jeremiah: Prophet of Courage and Hope.* Nashville: Abingdon Press, 1958.

Taylor, Charles L., Jr. "The Book of Habakkuk." In *The Interpreter's Bible,* edited by George A. Buttrick et al., vol. 6, 973-1003. Nashville: Abingdon Press, 1956.

Taylor, Charles L., Jr. "The Book of Nahum." In *The Interpreter's Bible,* edited by George A. Buttrick et al., vol. 6, 953-979. Nashville: Abingdon Press, 1956.

Taylor, Charles L., Jr. "The Book of Zephaniah." In *The Interpreter's Bible,* edited by George A. Buttrick et al., vol. 6, 1007-1034. Nashville: Abingdon Press, 1956.

Thompson, J. A. *The Book of Jeremiah.* The New International Commentary on the Old Testament, vol. 24. Grand Rapids: William B. Eerdmans, 1980.

9

THE EXILIC PROPHETS

Ezekiel, Isaiah 40–55, Obadiah

The Fall of Jerusalem in 587 B.C. catapulted large numbers of Judeans, particularly the leadership and artisans, into captivity in Babylonia. Perhaps the word "captivity" is misleading, since most of the people were probably not slaves. Jeremiah's letter to the exiles indicates that they were able to continue in their regular lives and occupations (29:1-32), and Ezekiel shows that they could move about freely (8:1; 20:1). Still they were displaced persons; they faced new political and religious influences. Yet it should not be thought that the entire nation was deported. Apparently only a small percentage of the population was taken away (see 2 Kings 24:14-16; Jeremiah 52:28-30). The majority remained in the shattered land (Lamentations; Obadiah), or else they emigrated to other lands, such as Egypt (Jeremiah 43–44). The significance of the exiles in Babylonia, therefore, did not lie in their numbers, but in their make-up; as we have seen, the majority of the leaders was taken off by Nebuchadnezzar. So this was an extremely crucial time for the Jews. Dispersed, dejected, and with their leadership stripped of its power, they needed strong voices to help them maintain their unity and religious commitment and to provide some guidance for the future. We have preserved for us the words of two prophets who arose in Babylonia during this period—Ezekiel and Second Isaiah (chapters 40–55). Another record comes from a prophet who remained in Judah—the Book of Obadiah. All three come from the period of the exile, that is, between 587 B.C. and the return from exile after the capture of Babylonia by the Persians in 539 B.C. These books show that the form of prophecy had begun to change. The preexilic prophets were largely persons of the spoken word. They moved about the country delivering their oracles, and these messages were then remembered and recorded at a later time (see Isaiah 8:1; Jeremiah 36). But now the written word began to gain in importance as a vehicle of communication, although the spoken word was still used. This development probably was largely due to the political situation in which it was not as effective to move about as spokespersons of Yahweh.

THE BOOK OF EZEKIEL

There is no question that Ezekiel is one of the most fascinating of the prophets, largely because of his strange personality and his use of imagery. The "wheel within a wheel" (chapter 1), the "valley of the dry bones" (chapter 37), and the battle with "Gog from the land of Magog" (chapters 38–39) have all been made very familiar by song and art and preaching. Yet the Book of Ezekiel is not read much, and the prophet has been too harshly judged.

1. The Historical Setting. Ezekiel began his ministry among the exiled Jews in Babylonia. He had been a priest in Jerusalem during the troubled days following the death of King Josiah at the hands of the Egyptians (609 B.C.). Domination by the Egyptians had followed until their defeat by the Babylonians (605 B.C.). The nation of Judah then became a vassal of Babylonia (Jeremiah 46:2ff.), and King Jehoiakim swore allegiance. Later Jehoiakim rebelled by refusing to pay tribute (2 Kings 24:1), and so Nebuchadnezzar sent Babylonian troops against Jerusalem. In 597 B.C. the city fell. Jehoiakim's eighteen-year-old son and successor, Jehoichin, took the brunt of the invasion. He, the queen mother, the leading officials, citizens, and artisans were taken to Babylon as captives (2 Kings 24). Ezekiel was among this group of captives. In Palestine the nation continued, if only temporarily, under the uncle of Jehoiachin, Zedekiah, who had been appointed by the Babylonians (2 Kings 24:17). Jeremiah was preaching at this time and attempting to keep King Zedekiah loyal to Babylonia. For a while he was successful, but in 588 B.C. the king revolted (2 Kings 24:20). The result was as Jeremiah had expected. The Babylonian armies once again appeared, and in 587 B.C. the city walls were breached. Great slaughter resulted; the city was plundered; the temple and the palace were set on fire, and the walls were destroyed (2 Kings 25; Lamentations). Zedekiah attempted to flee, but he was captured. After being forced to watch his sons killed, he was blinded and taken to Babylon where he died (2 Kings 25:6-7; Jeremiah 52:9-11).

2. The Prophet. Ezekiel tells us that he settled among a community of exiles at Tel-Abib by the River Chebar (1:1-3; 3:15), and after five years (593 B.C.) he received Yahweh's call to be a prophet (1–3). There he labored until 571 B.C. (29:17). Ezekiel no longer functioned as a priest, since the practice of Jewish cultic worship was forbidden in Babylonia, particularly because Babylonia was an unclean land and there was no temple. He lived in his own house, and apparently he did not undertake the usual prophetic role of moving about with the word of the Lord. Instead the people came to him, and there they listened to his words (3:24; 8:1; 12:3ff; 14:1; 20:1).

3. The Message. Ezekiel had to face a captured people, cruelly buoyed up by false hopes of a quick return to Palestine (see 13:1-23), and had to try to make them look at life realistically by focusing on the meaning of two events—the destruction of Jerusalem (1–24) and the restoration of Israel (25–48). The basic theme of the first event is that Jerusalem's doom and the continued exile of the people were inescapable. It was too late to repent (7:1-27). The second event is described as preceded by the destruction of the surrounding nations (25–32), which will then pave the way for the "dry bones" of Israel to come back to life (33–39) and for the temple and the land to be restored (40–48).

In the midst of this, Ezekiel had to combat a general feeling among the people that God had treated them rather shabbily. It is epitomized in their words: "The way of the LORD is not just" (33:17). So, in a sense, the book revolves around Ezekiel's response to this general mood. He seeks to establish proof that Yahweh is not unjust by appealing to two arguments.

First, Ezekiel reviews Israel's history to prove that as a matter of fact Israel had practiced idolatry, had been rebellious from the very beginning in Egypt, and had remained rebellious to that very day (20:1-32; see 16:23). For these reasons Israel was justifiably stripped of its possessions as a woman caught in adultery (23).

Second, he stresses that all people are responsible for themselves, and therefore by their own decisions determine their future. The people had been attempting to excuse themselves by quoting an old proverb: "The fathers have eaten sour grapes, and the children's teeth are set on edge" (18:2; see Jeremiah 31:29). Perhaps the parents had sinned, but it is unjust to punish the children for their crimes. This was the people's argument. In 2 Kings 21:10-15 the fall of Jerusalem is claimed as punishment for the sins of King Manasseh. There is truth in this approach: All people participate in social life, and inevitably they share in the decisions of the leadership. But Ezekiel knew that the people were simply looking for an excuse, that they were not free of sin themselves, and so he sought to combat that particular mood at that particular time by enunciating, and in the process overstating, the doctrine of individual responsibility. He spells this out particularly in chapters 18 and 33:10-20. Children, says Ezekiel, are not held guilty for the sins of their parents, nor does the righteousness of parents affect their children. "All souls are mine; the soul of the father as well as the soul of the son is mine: the soul that sins shall die" (18:4). Thus it is up to individuals to choose their own lives and destinies. Now this doctrine of individual responsibility is wrong if taken absolutely literally, and certainly Ezekiel knew this. He even speaks elsewhere of little children sharing in the destruction (9:6). The prophet is speaking to the particular problem of despondency and of a sense of uselessness among the exiles. So he seeks to encourage them that individual effort is worthwhile and that all persons can share in a glorious future by their own decision. People are not slaves to the past either in terms of their heredity or in terms of the actions of their forebears. People can determine their own future (18:21-23; 33:11). The prophet has a balance that is often lacking in contemporary discussion. People are influenced and affected by the past, but not to the exclusion of present freedom of choice. The important thing is to determine what creative actions can be done in the present; the past cannot be changed. Here the prophet has something profound to say to any age, even though the form of his expectation regarding the future was uniquely related to his own time in history.

THE BOOK OF ISAIAH (CHAPTERS 40–55)

The unknown author, usually called "Second Isaiah," wrote during the last days of the Babylonian empire, just before it came crashing down under the armed might of the Persians. In one of the most brilliant pieces of poetry in the entire Old Testament, Second Isaiah saw the crash coming and dealt with its implications for Israel and for the world.

1. The Historical Setting. The prophet Isaiah in the eighth century (chapters 1–39) had spoken of Assyria as the world power that Yahweh would use to punish the people of God (10:5-15). We have already seen the details of this. In 612 B.C. the Assyrian capital of Nineveh fell before the Babylonians and the Medes, and eventually most of the old Assyrian empire came under the control of the Babylonians. In the process of consolidating their gains, the Babylonians destroyed Jerusalem and carried off many captives to Babylonia. However, the Babylonians also felt the inexorable crush of history. In 550 B.C. the Persians, under an enlightened leader named Cyrus, embarked on a series of conquests. After overrunning various surrounding nations, Cyrus entered the gate of Babylon in 539 B.C. and established the Persian rule. Once again a prophet saw the hand of Yahweh in the movements of a foreign power. This time, however, Yahweh was not using a nation to punish Israel, but rather to deliver it (40:1-2). Second Isaiah spoke of Cyrus as the Lord's "anointed" (if we use the Greek translation, he was Yahweh's "Messiah"), sent to fulfill God's purposes, particularly in reference to Israel's restoration (44:28–45:1). Indeed, Ezra records for us the actual decrees of Cyrus that authorized the Israelites to return to Palestine (Ezra 1:1-4; 6:3-5). It is against this historical background that Isaiah 40–55 must be read.

2. The Message. Second Isaiah is a frustrating book to attempt to outline or divide into major units. It soon becomes apparent that the present chapter divisions artificially separate the ideas. Some scholars have felt that the book is similar to most of the other prophetic works in being a collection of various independent oracles unrelated to each other. Others have claimed that it is composed of separate poems, but that these have been arranged into an overall whole. However, no two scholars can agree on where separate poems end and new ones begin. As one reads the book, the striking impression gained is that the whole is a unity, with each thought leading into the other. So perhaps it is best to consider the book as a continuous essay, probably originally written with certain basic ideas repeated, expanded, and interwoven with other concepts.

The book does have a structure, even though it is a broad one. Chapter 40 is clearly the introduction, for it contains brief mention of the two basic themes with which chapters 41–54 are concerned—the pardon of Israel coupled with the coming of Cyrus (41–48) and the restoration of Israel coupled with the establishment of God's rule (49–54). Chapter 55 is then the conclusion as it presents a great hymn of triumph celebrating the coming mighty acts of Yahweh and the certainty of restoration (see especially 55:10-11). Many scholars feel that chapter 35 also belongs in this section, perhaps after chapter 55, although its original place is not clear.

It will be helpful in reading to note that throughout the book Second Isaiah stresses two important theological ideas. *First,* Yahweh is the only God, Creator, Savior, Lord of history and nature. *Second,* Yahweh's people Israel have been called for a worldwide mission, and they have been delivered from Babylonia and restored to the land so that they might fulfill that divine purpose for all people. These two ideas are proclaimed initially and summarily in chapter 40 and then expanded in detail throughout the rest of chapters 41–55. The first idea is clear enough (see 40:21-27; 41:4; 42:5), but the second idea has had a great deal of discussion. It concerns Second Isaiah's references to the role of a "servant" in the purposes of God. This servant has a mission both to Israel (49:5) and to the world (42:4; 49:6). It is difficult, however, to know when the text is speaking of the servant and who is being described. In regard to the "when," the usual position has been that there are four passages, called the "servant songs," which speak of this figure of the servant, that were inserted later into the text by unknown hands (42:1-4; 49:1-6; 50:4-9; 52:13–53:12) and that describe a different servant from the "servant Israel" mentioned elsewhere (for example, 41:8; 44:1-2; 45:4). Others, particularly those who see the book as a unified treatise, argue that these passages were not added to the text and are an integral part of the whole essay. With reference to the "who" question, there have been many suggestions. Scholars have suggested three basic interpretations: (1) *Collective*—The servant is actual Israel, ideal Israel, or a remnant within Israel. (2) *Individual*—The servant is a historical individual (Moses, Isaiah, Hezekiah, Jehoiachin, Jeremiah, and so forth), or a contemporary person (some unknown religious leader known to the prophet, or Second Isaiah himself), or a future figure (the Messiah or some prophet). (3) *Combination*—The servant combines elements relating both to the suffering mission of Israel and to an individual who uniquely accomplishes that suffering mission. Traditionally the church has assumed that the "servant" was Jesus Christ.

What is the solution to the problem of the identity of the servant? The history of debate on this subject should warn us about responding: "Here is *the* solution." However, certain facts seem more plausible than others. *First,* the servant is clearly identified as Israel in various passages (41:8; 42:18-19; 44:1-2), as well as in one of the "servant songs" (49:3). In the latter passage some scholars would omit the word "Israel" from the text, considering it a later addition, even though there is no textual evidence for this. It would seem strange that a different servant would be meant in the other "servant songs" unless some explicit statement to this effect were made. There is, therefore, one servant throughout—Israel. *Second,* various passages state that the servant is the recipient of salvation (40:1-2; 41:8), but in the servant songs the servant brings salvation to others (42:1-4; 49:5-6). This identification of two roles, it would seem, does not mean two different servants, as some think, but it is rather a description of two aspects of Israel's life—delivered from exile in order to undertake a mission to the world. Thus, even when the task of the servant is "to bring Jacob back to him, and that Israel might be gathered to him" (49:5), this is merely an illustration of the fact that Israel also has a mission to itself. Israel has always been both rebel (43:27; 48:8) and servant (44:2; 59:21) at the same time. Therefore, it is appropriate to speak of Israel's mission as partly to encourage its own people to fulfill their calling. *Third,* there are, however, apparent differences between the description of the servant in 52:13–53:12 and in the rest of the book. Elsewhere in the book the servant suffers because of faithfulness to the mission (for example, 50:6), but here the servant suffers in order to fulfill the mission (for example, 53:10-12). On the one hand, the servant suffers because of humanity's sin, but, on the other, the servant also suffers for the sake of humanity's sin (53:5). Isaiah 42:18-25 speaks of the just punishment of Israel, but 53:9 speaks of unjust punishment of the servant. Who then is the servant here? Could it still be Israel? It would seem that the best solution is to identify the servant as a "corporate personality." The description of the servant in Second Isaiah is a "combined" description containing elements that apply, on the one hand, to God's people, called to suffer in faithfulness so that the world might find God (41:11-13; 42:1-9) and, on the other hand, to some individual among the people who supremely carries out the mission in a way no one else can—the servant, though not deserving to suffer, suffers redemptively for the rest of humanity. The servant passages—all of them—tell us that God's purpose is that through the suffering of this "servant" the world will be made whole.

The portrait of that servant has been painted large enough to include all in the past, present, and future (including Jesus Christ) who undertake that task. Each description in the passages does not apply to each individual servant throughout history, but all descriptions together make up the "servant of the LORD." This comes clear when we consider the New Testament. On the one hand, it sees Jesus as the individual who suffered redemptively and uniquely to reconcile humanity to God. It even uses the language of Isaiah 53 to describe him (Mark 10:45; Luke 22:37; 1 Corinthians 15:3; Acts 8:26-39). The picture in Isaiah 52–53 is thus a remarkable anticipation of the sufferings of Jesus. Yet the description is not a prediction of Jesus, for there is much in the passage that cannot apply to him, for example, "no form or comeliness" (53:2) or "made his grave with the wicked" (53:9). On the other hand, the New Testament sees the people of God as the suffering servant (2 Corinthians 1:5; Philippians 3:10; 1 Peter 4:13), even completing "what is lacking in Christ's afflictions" (Colossians

1:24), who will be a "light to the world" (Matthew 5:14; compare Isaiah 42:6; 49:6) as Jesus was the "light" (John 1:9). Thus, Second Isaiah has not given a detailed delineation of any one person, but a broad picture of the servant whom God intends to use for worldwide mission. Israel is that servant, the church is that servant, and so is Jesus; each contributes in a unique way. This message of the divine purpose in suffering, therefore, must have helped Second Isaiah's contemporaries come to recognize that their own plight was not only to be viewed as punishment for sin, but as an opportunity to enter into the purposes of God in the present and in the future.

THE BOOK OF OBADIAH

This intriguing little book, the shortest in the Old Testament, is ascribed simply to Obadiah (that is, servant of Yahweh). The name is common in the Old Testament, occurring twelve times. Whether or not it refers in this book to an actual prophet is uncertain. It may only be a synonym for "prophet" because the book appears to be a collection of anonymous oracles delivered in Jerusalem during the grim days after its fall in 587 B.C. The oracles deal with a common theme: Edom. We find others against Edom elsewhere in the prophetic books (for example, Amos 1:11-12; Jeremiah 49:7-22). Furthermore, there are marked similarities both in phraseology and ideas between Obadiah 1-8 and Jeremiah 49:7-16. So we do not know anything about the author or authors.

The hatred expressed towards Edom is typical of the hostility that existed between Israel and Edom through the years. It began with the struggle between the two ancestors of the tribes, Jacob and Esau (Genesis 25:19-34), and continued throughout the Old Testament period. In the sixth and fifth centuries B.C. the old enmity found expression (Isaiah 63:1-6; Ezekiel 25:12-14; Lamentations 4:21; Psalm 137:7; Malachi 1:2-5). The particular evils singled out are found in verses 10-14: refusing to help Judah during the siege by Nebuchadnezzar (11-12), joining in the looting of Jerusalem (13), and helping the Babylonians capture the fleeing refugees (14). The spirit that permeates the book and its promises of judgment and restoration is not a simple naive nationalism, but a thoroughly Old Testament faith that views history as inevitably and eventually in the control of Yahweh. Consequently, evil brings its own punishment:

> For the day of the LORD is near upon all the nations.
> As you have done, it shall be done to you,
> your deeds shall return on your own head.
> —Obadiah 15

Yet the Book of Obadiah illustrates for us, by its fierce desire for the annihilation of the Edomites, the fact that logical theology often goes hand in hand with human hate.

- How may we summarize Ezekiel's mission to the exiles? What did he consider to be the major elements in the kingdom of God? How has the New Testament reinterpreted these things? What does all this say about our expectations of the form of God's future work in the world?
- What was Israel's mission according to Second Isaiah? If the church is the new Israel (Galatians 6:16), what implications does the prophet's message have for its role in society? (see Isaiah 42:1-7; 49:1-6).
- What part does the prophetic affirmation about God's sovereignty over history play in our faith and in the way we live? Does it mean that we cannot expect to change our world?

Additional Resources

Eichrodt, Walther. *Ezekiel: A Commentary.* Philadelphia: Westminster Press, 1970.

May, Herbert G. "The Book of Ezekiel." In *The Interpreter's Bible,* edited by George A. Buttrick et al., vol. 6, 41-338. Nashville: Abingdon Press, 1956.

Muilenburg, James. "The Book of Isaiah, Chapters 40–66." In *The Interpreter's Bible,* edited by George A. Buttrick et al., vol. 5, 381-773. Nashville: Abingdon Press, 1956.

Watts, John D. *Obadiah: A Critical Exegetical Commentary.* Grand Rapids: William B. Eerdmans, 1969.

Westermann, Claus. *Isaiah 40–66.* Translated by David M. Stalker. Philadelphia: Westminster Press, 1969.

Whybray, R. N. *Isaiah 40–66.* New Century Bible Commentary. Grand Rapids: William B. Eerdmans, 1981.
Wolff, H. W. *Obadiah and Jonah: A Commentary.* Translated by Margaret Kohl. Minneapolis: Augsburg, 1986.

10

THE POSTEXILIC PROPHETS

Isaiah 56–66, Joel, Jonah, Haggai, Zechariah, Malachi

After the return from exile in 538 B.C., there was still need for a divine word both for those who had made the journey home and for those who grew up after them. This "postexilic" period dates from 538 B.C. to the close of the Old Testament historical record in the last few centuries before Christ. The glorious promises of Second Isaiah about the restoration of land and life did not materialize the way that was expected. We saw in the study of Ezra and Nehemiah how drought and famine sapped the initiative of the returnees to rebuild the temple and the walls of Jerusalem. The foreigners who had settled in the land during the exile saw the returned Jews as possible threats to their own position and safety, and so they tried to block even the feeble attempts at reconstruction. The Persian overlords allowed the Jews to enjoy a measure of autonomy and to maintain their own customs and religious practices. Cyrus had even tried to encourage rebuilding the temple by returning the sacred vessels that had been taken by Nebuchadnezzar (Ezra 1:7-11). But the Jews were slow to respond. Finally the temple (515 B.C.) and the city walls (444 B.C.) were rebuilt, largely under the impetus supplied by various prophets. Even after these rebuilding measures, however, life had to go on, often in the face of discouragements and hardships. What had happened to God's great promises? The prophets also had to speak to this. The Old Testament historical record ends around 400 B.C. in the events described in the books of Ezra and Nehemiah. From allusions in some of the postexilic prophets and from extra-biblical sources, we know that Persian rule gave way to Greek in 331 B.C. The details of this period are extremely sketchy, and it is not until the second century B.C. when the Jews achieved independence for a brief period (142–63 B.C.) that we learn much more. The Romans conquered the Jews in 63 B.C., and not until modern times did the Jews ever again become an independent state. We shall look at those few years of struggle for independence in the second century B.C. when we consider the book of Daniel.

THE BOOK OF ISAIAH (CHAPTERS 56–66)

1. The Historical Setting. Traditionally these chapters have been assumed to be the last part of the message of the eighth century prophet Isaiah, but contemporary scholarship has shown us, on the basis of differences in style, contents, and outlook, that (a) they come from Second Isaiah, or (b) they are the product of a later unknown prophet (Third Isaiah), or (c) they are a collection of messages from various prophets who lived in Palestine during the period between 587 and 400 B.C. For many scholars there is no question that the geographical situation reflected in these chapters is Palestine, and not Babylon, and that the primary historical setting is postexilic. It is also clear that the nature of the materials is different from Second Isaiah. While the latter is an extended, apparently written, essay, chapters 56–66 are a collection of spoken oracles and prayers that were uttered in the normal prophetic fashion (for example, 56:8). In essence, they attack various pagan practices (57:1-13) and sins (59:1-15*a*) in Judah that hinder the completion of God's purposes and also provide reassurance that God's full salvation will eventually come (59:15*b*-21; 60–63; 65–66). It may be that Second Isaiah spoke these messages, or at least some of them, after his return from captivity. The similarity, for example, between 57:14-21 and 40:1-4, or between 60–62 and 40–55, is striking. Yet there are historical differences that make a complete identification with Second Isaiah difficult. In 63:7–64:12 the author speaks of a burned temple and of land destroyed by foreigners (for example, 63:18; 64:11) in a way that suggests a time shortly after the fall of Jerusalem in 587 B.C. Yet 56:1-8 and 60:7, 13 imply that the temple is standing and in use (that is, after 515 B.C.). In 62:10-12 the people in Jerusalem are charged to prepare for the coming return of the exiles, and the expressions used are in some cases identical to the charge given by Second Isaiah to the people in exile as they faced their own return (40:9-11). So it is perhaps best to see in chapters 56–66 a collection of materials from various prophets, including Second Isaiah, that deal with the struggles of the people in Palestine during the days immediately after the destruction by the Babylonians (587 B.C.) through the time of return (538 B.C.) and on into the period of reconstruction. Thus, although the problem rather consistently concerns the future of God's people, the background to these chapters varies.

2. The Message. There is no particular structure, but interlaced throughout the chapters is the theme of hope. It is not a hope, however, that is based on simple, passive waiting for God to act. As is true so often in the Old Testament, it is hope conditioned by Israel's loyal response to the divine will. Yahweh will not work apart from Israel. This note is sounded in the opening words:

> Thus says the LORD:
> "Keep justice, and do righteousness,
> for soon my salvation will come,
> and my deliverance be revealed."
> —Isaiah 56:1

In other words, the Lord will not provide salvation to those who refuse to obey its conditions. The people had become bitterly disappointed with the apparent failure of the divine promises. To this kind of despair a prophet responded:

> Behold, the LORD's hand is not
> shortened, that it cannot save,
> or his ear dull, that it cannot hear. . . .
> —Isaiah 59:1

The book then spells out the divine terms for national restoration and stability.

Two basic requirements are proclaimed throughout these chapters—proper observance of worship regulations, particularly regarding the sabbath (56:2; 58:13-14; 65:1-12), and consistent moral conduct in all of life (58:1-12; 59:3-21). The emphasis on the sabbath is characteristic of postexilic Judaism, for it had become a special symbol of one's allegiance to the Lord during the days when there was no temple. But the heart of the divine requirement that demonstrated one's allegiance was concern for Yahweh's will in social affairs. The words of 58:6-9 are especially significant. As Sheldon Blank writes, "Hope is not so much a heavenly gift as a divine requirement."[10] This concern is not simply prophetic theologizing, but a profound political reality. A nation is only secure and stable when it establishes social conditions that really provide for these things. God does not give peace if people will not do their part. If people are responsive, the book gives a dramatic promise. Using the imagery of later apocalyptic writings (for example, Daniel), the book promises a world to be established by Yahweh that can only be described as "new heavens and a new earth" (65:17), where there will be felicity unimagined (60:1-7; 65:17-25; 66:22-23), and where the everlasting and constant presence of Yahweh will do away with the need for illumination (60: 19-20). The ultimate fulfillment of this lay beyond the understanding of the Israelites, but the author of the Revelation to John in the New Testament utilized this terminology when speaking of heaven where "night shall be no more" (Revelation 22:5).

THE BOOK OF JOEL

The Book of Joel comes out of the midst of national disaster—drought and locust plague. The country of Judah has been stripped of its crops by hordes of locusts, and this has been followed by a drought that has completed the devastation. Joel seeks to get the people to make this disaster an occasion for a serious reevaluation of their lives. He feels that these plagues warn of an impending doom, the day of the Lord.

1. The Historical Setting. The exact historical situation of these events is unknown. The superscription to the book tells us nothing except the name of the prophet and his father. The contents and style are historically ambiguous. Scholars have dated the book variously between the ninth and the fourth centuries B.C. The best that can be said is that the weight of evidence suggests the postexilic period. There is no condemnation of the social and religious evils so typical of the preexilic prophets. No king is mentioned among the leadership (1:5-14); the destruction of Judah by the

Babylonians and the dispersion of the people have taken place in the past (3:2), the temple has been rebuilt (1:9, 14, 16; 2:17), and the walls of Jerusalem have been restored (2:7, 9). All this is described in language that is very colorful, but it is characteristic of apocalyptic writing from the last centuries before Jesus Christ. This evidence would thus indicate a date somewhere near the close of the fifth century or the beginning of the fourth B.C. Establishing the exact date, however, is not of importance, for the significance of the book derives from the kind of setting more than from the specific occasion.

2. The Message. The book falls clearly into two parts. *First,* in chapters 1:2–2:27 the prophet seeks to draw out the theological significance of the natural disasters. The unparalleled devastation of the land by locusts and drought can only mean, says Joel, that Yahweh is warning the people about a larger event. They are harbingers that the great "day of the LORD" is near, the "day" when Yahweh would establish the final purposes for Israel and the nations. Notice the dramatic way the prophet spells this out (1:15–2:11), similar to the "communal prayer in time of trouble" found throughout the book of Psalms (for example, Psalms 12, 44). This has led some scholars to suggest that the book was performed as a liturgy in the temple. This section concludes with the claim of the prophet that there is only one way to avert complete tragedy—sincere repentance by the whole nation, for "who knows whether he will not turn and repent, and leave a blessing behind him . . ." (2:14). This is followed by a promise (2:18-27) that in the day of judgment a repentant Israel will be answered by Yahweh with a restoration of fertility (2:19-25) and of life (2:26-27).

The *second* part of the book (2:28–3:21) takes the promise of restoration for Judah from the plague and projects it on a worldwide scale. The "day of the LORD" will mean spiritual transformation, unimagined natural felicity for Israel, and subjugation of all of Israel's enemies. The imagery is suggestive of the kind of symbolism found in abundance in later apocalyptic literature, such as the Book of Daniel. The gift of the spirit in 2:28-29 will mean that "all flesh" (here this means all Israel) will become prophets, for "dreams" and "visions" are allusions to the way the prophets received their messages from Yahweh. Thus, all God's people, not just chosen individuals, will enter into a unique prophetic ministry. Perhaps there are also overtones of that which is expressed in Jeremiah 31:31-34 and Ezekiel 36:26-27. The New Testament makes the promise universal so that it refers to all people, not just Israelites, who confess faith in God (Acts 2:1-21) and who are thus charged to a worldwide mission of proclaiming the gospel (Acts 1:8). In this way the original mission of "Israel" will be fulfilled (Genesis 12:3; Isaiah 42:1-9). What Joel dimly saw, therefore, as a sign of the messianic age is given greater clarity and scope in the Acts of the Apostles. Furthermore, what the prophet proclaimed regarding God's sovereignty over all the forces of life, natural and political and personal, and what he knew to be the basis for entrance into God's blessings—repentance and commitment—were to have a fulfillment which he could only imperfectly imagine. Joel was a child of his times and his geographical situation in his distinction between Israel and the rest of humanity and in his description of the natural wonders of the kingdom of God. The fulfillment of God's promises was to change the form in which Joel expected them, but the prophet was right about the God who fulfilled them.

THE BOOK OF JONAH

One of the most profound Old Testament books, Jonah, has been one of the most superficially used. The emphasis so often has been directed towards the great fish. Could a whale really swallow a human being? Could a person survive in the belly of a whale? Did this really happen? These are common questions. Scholarship has shown us that the fish story is really only the embroidery around the edge of quite a different concern.

1. The Literary Form. The book is unique among the Latter Prophets, for it is primarily a narrative (a report) about the prophet Jonah in the midst of which has been inserted a prayer (2:1-9), words directed to God. There is no record of Jonah's message apart from the brief words in 3:4: "Yet forty days, and Nineveh shall be overthrown."

The story is clear, but not the literary form. There have been many suggestions. Is it history, allegory, parable, or what? Traditionally the book has been thought to be a *historical narrative.* We know that the prophet Jonah was a historical figure, for 2 Kings 14:25 tells us that Jonah predicted the expansion of Israel's borders during the reign of Jeroboam II (786–746 B.C.); but this is all we learn. It may be that Jonah was carried captive into Assyria when a little later (733–732 B.C.) Tiglath-pileser, king of Assyria, recaptured some of his lost territory (2 Kings 15:29; 17:6). Does this, however, mean the book is a historical narrative? Not necessarily, for historical figures and groups have been used elsewhere in the Bible in allegories (Isaiah 5:1-7; Galatians 4:21-31) and parables (Luke 16:19-31). Even the use by the Jews (Tobit 14:8) and Jesus (Matthew 12:40-41) does not prove historicity since both were using a teaching out of the book and would not have been interested in arguing the historical questions. Many scholars have pointed out historical difficulties in the book—the size of Nineveh (archaeology has shown it was quite a bit smaller than Jonah describes: "three days' journey in breadth," 3:3; "a hundred and twenty thousand" children, 4:11), the swift and wide-scale conversion of the city, the plant and worm incident, as well as the swallowing of Jonah by the great fish. Furthermore, the prayer in 2:1-9 is inappropriate in its context, and it appears to have been added later. It is a thanksgiving for deliverance from death unrelated to the fish, and it is offered in the temple (2:7).

Some have felt that the book is an *allegory* about Israel (Jonah), who was called on a mission to the nations and who sought to run away and subsequently was swallowed up by Babylonia (the great fish) for seventy years (the three days and nights in the belly of the fish). One scholar even suggested that the "great fish" was the name of a ship that rescued Jonah![11] But aside from the fact that in the book the fish saved Jonah from drowning, and thus is inappropriate to Babylonia, there are many other details that cannot be given logical allegorical meanings. Thus, another interpretation must be sought.

It seems best, with most scholars, to classify the book either as a *parable* (a short story with a moral, similar to the parables of Jesus) or else as a *midrash* (a story that seeks to make a biblical person or event relevant for a later age by rewriting and expanding the details by means of elements drawn from folklore). In either case, the historical question is therefore irrelevant since the emphasis is on the religious lesson. The purpose is not to present history, but to enhance the theological point by exaggeration and popular incidents. Jesus' use of "Abraham's bosom" is an example of this in Luke 12:19-31. We know that most of the miraculous elements in the story of Jonah, including the swallowing of a man by a sea monster, were very widespread in ancient literature and tradition. It is useless, therefore, to argue over the possibility of whether or not a whale could swallow a human being and whether a person could remain alive in such circumstances. There was a historical figure of the eighth century B.C. named Jonah, but this book uses him as the occasion to proclaim a theological lesson to a people in a later age. This is similar to the book of Ecclesiastes with its use of Solomon. The language, vocabulary, and contents suggest that Jonah was written sometime around the fifth century B.C., long after Nineveh had been destroyed (612 B.C.) and when its size had been forgotten.

2. The Message. What is the book's purpose? A common explanation is that the book is a protest against the exclusivism of the policies of Ezra and Nehemiah, who sought to exclude all foreigners from the midst of the postexilic community. This may have been a secondary concern, but the dominant thrust of the book is more positive. It shares with Second Isaiah a charge to restored Israel to become the servant of the Lord and to fulfill its mission to the world for which it was called (Isaiah 42:1-9). The emphasis of the book is on God's graciousness to all people, even to the hated enemies of Israel. In Jonah's reluctance to undertake the call—he even preferred to die rather than to go to Nineveh (1:12) or to have the people saved (4:3)—Israel was to read its own selfishness and insularity. Israel was being warned not to believe, as it had so often, that its choice as God's own people (Exodus 19:6) meant that Israel alone merited the attention and love of Yahweh.

The book, therefore, stressed, *first,* that God was graciously concerned for the salvation of all people. It thus spoke to the particularism of the kind found in some of the prophets (for example, Joel) who uttered eschatological threats regarding the destruction of all nations and concerning promises about the salvation only of Israel. *Second,* it also emphasized that Yahweh continued to work through God's servants even when they had been disobedient and reluctant. Jonah was given a second chance to be God's servant. So the book (like the Chronicler) taught that there was a continuity between postexilic Israel and the preexilic promises and intentions of Yahweh. The exile had not destroyed the covenant or the call. *Finally,* the book showed that nothing, not even Israel's refusal, could ultimately thwart the fulfillment of Yahweh's universal purpose to save humankind. The book was thus a fit preparation for the universalistic message of God's love brought by Jesus Christ.

THE BOOK OF HAGGAI

1. The Historical Setting. This is one of those books that at first reading is dull and provincial, but after closer examination reveals profundity of insight. The prophet Haggai, also mentioned in Ezra 5:1; 6:14, had apparently been among the exiles in Babylonia and was part of the leadership in postexilic days. His dated ministry is not long, for as the sequence of chronological information shows us (1:1, 15; 2:1, 10, 20), he labored only from August to December, 520 B.C. These were crisis days, as was usually the case when the prophets arose. The Jews had recently returned from Babylonia (538 B.C.) and had experienced a series of natural and political troubles. They were still vassals to the Persians, and the glories promised by Second Isaiah had not materialized. Something, however, happened on the political scene in 522 B.C. that began to awaken Jewish hopes. The Persian ruler Cambyses committed suicide over a palace intrigue, and at his death a general revolt broke out around his empire. Various pretenders to the Persian throne fought for control, and the future of the kingdom was very uncertain. This instability caused nationalistic hopes to be enflamed in the small vassal countries, including Judah. Now the old prophetic promises began to be revived. Was this the beginning of the end for the pagan nations and the start of God's kingdom? It was in this situation of excitement and expectation that Haggai ministered. He sought to challenge the people to rebuild the temple as quickly as possible, for Yahweh was in the process of bringing in the kingdom. Four years later the temple was built (515 B.C.), but the kingdom did not come. The Persians, under Darius Hystaspis, were able to reestablish a stable government towards the close of 520 B.C., and perhaps this is the reason that the prophet concluded his work at that time.

2. The Message. The book divides into five oracles, each of which is dated (1:1-15*a;* 1:15*b*–2:9; 2:10-14; 2:15-19; 2:20-23). But these oracles do not, at first glance, seem to contain anything of theological relevance because they are so localized in interest and, indeed, are incorrect in their expectation of the imminent end of the age. The book has historical importance for depicting life in postexilic days, but does it have more value than this? Perhaps so.

First, Haggai's consuming interest in the rebuilding of the temple, though misdirected eschatalogically, was based on solid thinking. He claimed that true restoration could not take place without careful concern over worship; indeed, this was the precondition of the coming of Yahweh. This sounds strange against the background of the preexilic prophets. They had been strong in their condemnation of worship, stressing the need for social concern (for example, Amos 5:21-24). Jeremiah even claimed that Yahweh had not commanded sacrifice to be offered (Jeremiah 7:22). What is the meaning of the difference? As Gerhard von Rad has pointed out, the difference is explained by the different spiritual conditions of the people.[12] In the preexilic period the problem faced by the prophets was a people with too much concern for the temple and too little interest in the moral and spiritual actions in business and family life. To exemplify justice and honesty was the sign in those preexilic days that one took Yahweh seriously. But in the postexilic period, the people were so much involved in the day-to-day struggle with economic matters that they gave little concern to worship and God. Now to show zeal over the rebuilding of the temple was a sign that one was truly interested in the affairs of the Lord. The intent of the preexilic and postexilic prophets was the same—to encourage the people to take an active interest in the divine will—but the different situations meant different ways of expressing this.

Second, Haggai's interest in the temple was also based on a solid faith in the purposes of Yahweh. In his concentration on the rebuilding measures, Haggai was giving expression to his acknowledgment that Yahweh was at work in history. His contemporaries had given up hope; even when the restortion of the temple had started, it was "as nothing" in their sight (2:3). Israel's glory was in the past. Haggai had to proclaim to them that against all evidence Yahweh was beginning something new that would develop into a glory far brighter and with more universal implications than they had ever known (2:9). So, like Habakkuk (2:4), Haggai saw beyond the moment to the greater significance of events. All nations would worship Yahweh. That the prophet remained a fallible Israelite in the midst of this is clear from his expectation of an imminent future denouement with Zerubbabel as the Messiah. Yet so were other prophets tied to their own frailty in couching the future in strictly Israelite terms. But the fact that the books of Haggai and other prophets could become part of the canon even when their specific expectations had not come to pass shows that later Judaism and the church penetrated beyond the form of their words to see that people could still have hope in what was abiding in the prophetic message: faithfully, and in the mystery of Yahweh's own time and way, the promises would be fulfilled.

THE BOOK OF ZECHARIAH

The Book of Zechariah is best read when it is divided into three parts (1–8, 9–11, 12–14). Only the first part is from the prophet Zechariah, or at least only chapters 1–8 deal with the early postexilic period, as is indicated by the dates that span a period between 520 and 518 B.C. (1:1, 7; 7:1). The other two sections, although uncertain in many details, come from a later period, as stylistic differences and historical allusions show. These chapters contain no reference to the sixth century nor to Joshua or Zerubbabel, the two leaders during this time. They also refer to later historical circumstances, particularly during the time of the Greeks (for example, 9:13). Therefore, most scholars date them during the fifth to the third centuries B.C. and consider them to be two collections by anonymous prophets, each introduced by a common formula: "An oracle. The word of the LORD . . ." (9:1; 12:1). The Book of Malachi also begins this way, and, as we shall see, this may have been a third anonymous collection. All three were then added to the end of Zechariah, just as similar collections were appended to the Book of Isaiah (40–55, 56–66).

1. Zechariah 1–8.

a. *The historical setting.* This well-planned composition describes the ministry and words of the prophet Zechariah. He began his work one month before Haggai concluded (1:1; Haggai 2:10-14, 20-23) and continued for two more years. Thus, Zechariah arose when the political situation in Persia had been stabilized ("all the earth remains at rest"; 1:11) and when the temple was already in the process of being rebuilt. The great hopes in Judah, engendered by the unrest in Persia, had probably begun to die down. Zechariah sought to keep those hopes alive by showing, as Haggai had in his time, that historical circumstances were not always the clue to what Yahweh was doing. The prophet deals with the temple-building project, but he does not feel the need to admonish the people to continue the work. Instead, he looks forward with certainty to its completion, confident that its future is in the hands of God: "Not by might, nor by power, but by my Spirit, says the LORD of hosts" (4:6). Zechariah's major interest, however, is in the imminent eschatological age, the time of the establishment of God's kingdom. So he deals with various aspects of this, particularly with how Judah is to be organized and to conduct itself in this future which is near at hand.

b. *The prophet.* As is so often true among the prophets, not much is known about Zechariah. His name means "Yahweh remembers" or "Yahweh has remembered," and according to 1:1, 7 he was the son of Berachiah and the grandson of Iddo, the priest (Nehemiah 12:4, 16). Thus Zechariah, like Jeremiah and Ezekiel, was a prophet with a priestly heritage, and so he was an apt person to deal with the meaning of the temple. There is a problem, however, in that according to Ezra 5:1; 6:14, and Nehemiah 12:16, Zechariah was the *son* of Iddo, not his grandson. The explanation is probably that the phrase "the son of Berachiah" was incorrectly added by a later editor who confused him with a different Zechariah, the son of *Je*berachiah, mentioned in Isaiah 8:2.

c. *The message.* The book centers in a series of eight visions (1:7–6:8), which are preceded (1:1-6) and followed (6:9–8:23) by a collection of oracles by the prophet. They deal with a common theme—the great day of salvation that is now in the process of unfolding. Zechariah is much like Haggai in these chapters, although more colorful and interesting to read. The prophet, however, has his own contributions to make. *First,* in his concern over the rebuilding measures, his emphasis is not so much on the need to prepare in this way for the coming of Yahweh, although this element is found. Zechariah emphasizes, rather, the spiritual preparation of the people. They have been forgiven, and their sins will be taken away from them (3:9; 5:5-11). How this purification will take place is not made clear, but Zechariah clearly expects a radical change in human nature that will accompany the new age. This is reminiscent of Jeremiah and Ezekiel. The New Testament also sees this spiritual change at the coming of God's kingdom, but in ways unexpected by the Old Testament.

Second, Zechariah's teaching that historical circumstances are not always signs of God's activity was shared by Haggai, but the form that Zechariah gave to this is intriguing. He depicts divine agents, deliverers, events, and a kingdom already prepared in heaven and on the verge of bursting upon the world. Here the prophet draws on the imagery of his own time and place, for in Babylonian thought there was a pattern or original in heaven for everything on earth. In a similar way the tabernacle was patterned after a heavenly model (Exodus 25:9, 40). So here the prophet utilizes this kind of form to emphasize the fact that God's purposes for humanity have already been prepared. Zechariah was proclaiming to his contemporaries that the world was moving according to divine plan and was not out of control. Thus we read Zechariah as we read the whole Old Testament, keeping constantly aware of the differences between form and content. The prophet must use the imagery of his times to speak relevantly to the people, and the import of the message is lost or confused if the form of his words is taken as the reality he is expressing. It is true, of course, that the prophets did often assume that the form was the reality (for example, the expectation of a restored Jewish kingdom), but here Zechariah is simply affirming that the absence of apparent significance to life does not mean there is no significance nor that God is absent.

2. Zechariah 9–14. This section divides into two parts (9–11,

12–14) and provides a supplement by unknown authors to the prophecies of Zechariah. The formula in 9:1 and 12:1, without parallel in the prophets (except in Malachi 1:1), heads each division. There are many difficulties in the analysis and interpretation of the various passages, but they share a common theme with chapters 1–8, namely, the imminent arrival of the eschatological age with its glory for Israel and the subjugation of the nations. There is really no structure to these chapters, for they contain typical prophetic collections of oracles related only by a common concern over the establishment of the messianic reign. The dates or historical backgrounds to the separate oracles are extremely hard to determine. Furthermore, we find in these chapters more of the apocalyptic imagery than in earlier prophets, so detailed interpretation is out of the question. It is best for the reader to look for the general idea of the various sections and to avoid attempts at explicit identification of details.

a. *The historical setting.* If these prophecies come from the fifth to the third centuries B.C., as they apparently do, then they cover the last part of the Persian rule (538–331 B.C.) and the beginning of Greek domination (331–142 B.C.). Weakened by revolts among vassal nations and by court intrigues, Persia was unable to withstand the advance of Greek armies under Alexander the Great (336–323 B.C.). In 331 B.C. the empire changed hands. Alexander died in 323 B.C., having conquered the world, but his death brought a squabble among his generals, and his empire was divided among them. Palestine finally fell to his general Ptolemy and was ruled by Ptolemy and his descendants (301–198 B.C.). Unfortunately, we know almost nothing about events in Judah during this whole period nor about the fate of Jews scattered in other countries. Judah apparently continued to maintain a semi-independent existence under both Persian and Alexandrian rule, even to the extent of striking its own coins. There were contacts with other countries, as evidenced by inscriptions, coins, and other artifacts. Aramaic gradually began to replace Hebrew as the common language. Any events of significance, however, are not known. As John Bright says: "For the most part, the Jews seem to have been content to attend to their own affairs and to allow the march of history to pass them by."[13] This was to remain so until the second century B.C. when Seleucid Greeks wrested control of Palestine from Ptolemaic Greeks. We shall see the results of this in the discussion about the Book of Daniel.

b. *The message.* The oracles in Zechariah 9–14 must at present be interpreted without much link to historical circumstances. This is not as crucial as it might have been if the concern had not been with the eschatological age. The standard features of eschatological hope are here—the destruction of Israel's enemies, including the Greeks (9:1-8, 13; 12:1-9; 14:1-21), the coming of the messianic king (9:9-10), the regathering of the dispersed Israelites (9:11-17; 10:3-12), the purging of the nation's sin (12:1–13:6), and the establishment of Yahweh's universal dominion (14:1-21). Here, too, we notice typical Jewish nationalistic ideas, particularly in chapter 14. The closing verses betray an extremely narrow insistence that all the families of the earth must go to Jerusalem once a year or else suffer drought (14:16-17); Egypt is particularly threatened in this regard (14:18-19).

Two passages call for special notice. *First,* imbedded in chapter 9 is a brief oracle announcing the coming of Israel's prince of peace (9:9-10). The picture is of a victorious, righteous king riding into Jerusalem, about to reestablish a universal reign. The King James translation, "just and having salvation; lowly, and riding upon an ass," suggests a righteous but poor and afflicted figure entering Jerusalem. The Revised Standard rendering is better: "Triumphant and victorious is he, humble and riding on an ass. . . ." The emphasis in the first clause is on victory, while the last stresses royal righteousness. The word "humble" or "lowly" does not mean "having been humbled" or "oppressed" or "afflicted," but rather, as in the spirit of Micah 6:8, it conveys the meaning of "pious" or "reverent before God." Furthermore, riding on an ass did not signify humility but indicated royalty, since it was the normal mount of kings in ancient times (Judges 5:10; 10:4; 1 Kings 1:38, 44). The New Testament applied this passage to Jesus on Palm Sunday (Matthew 21:1-11). His appearance on an ass, a royal mount, excited messianic hopes.

Second, in 12:10-14 there is reference to some martyr whom the Jews in their wickedness have killed. In the eschatological age they will have a change of heart and mourn "him whom they have pierced" (12:10). The tendency of many has been to see a prediction of national repentance and conversion to Jesus Christ by the Jews. Indeed, Revelation 1:7 seems to apply the phrase to the Second Coming. But in context there is another reference. The "pierced one" is a prophet of the future who will be killed because people believe the prophet is a false prophet (see 13:3). Later, it will be discovered that he was a true prophet, and so there will be national mourning over his death and the people's failure to heed his words. What all this means, however, is not explained by Zechariah. In any case, the reference to Jesus Christ is at most analogical, for many of the details do not fit. Jesus used the wording of Zechariah 13:7 in a similar way to apply analogically to himself (Matthew 26:31). This passage, which includes 13:7-9, apparently reflects a realism regarding Israel's restoration. Zerubbabel had not become the Messiah after the return from Babylon. So the unknown author of 13:7-9 says that the leadership of Judah ("my shepherd") must again be removed and the people scattered before the real restoration and establishment will take place. This prediction is rather remarkable, but the despair of the unfulfilled years after the return from Babylonia must have led to this belief. Jesus uses this passage in quite a different context. Jesus would be struck, and the disciples would scatter. The following details in Zechariah 13:8-9, however, were not part of that analogy.

THE BOOK OF MALACHI

This little book was probably originally an appendix to Zechariah 1–8, along with Zechariah 9–11 and 12–14. We saw that each of these appendixes begins with the same formula, found only here in the prophets. The name "Malachi" may not actually be a proper name; it means "my messenger." It was perhaps taken by a later editor from 3:1 and assumed to be the name of the prophet. The reason the oracles were made into a separate book was in order to make twelve prophetic books, perhaps on the analogy of the twelve tribes.

1. The Historical Setting. The background to the book is the period around 450 B.C. The temple and cult have been restored (1:10; 3:1, 10), so the time of writing must be after Haggai and

Zechariah. There is also a carelessness in the conduct of worship (1:6-14; 2:1-9; 3:6-12), a flagrant use of the divorce provision (2:10-16), and a skepticism regarding God (3:13-15); so the book must date before the reforms of Ezra and Nehemiah. The people are therefore under Persian rule at a time when eschatological expectation, fanned by Haggai and Zecheriah, had died down. The kingdom had not come, and the people's disappointment is reflected throughout the book in their neglect of religious and moral obligation, and in their indifference to Yahweh.

2. The Message. The prophet's words are directed towards the physical and psychological situation of the time. Malachi speaks of the coming of the kingdom of God (2:17–3:5; 3:13–4:3) but does not attempt, like Haggai and Zechariah, to set a date or identify the Messiah. This would not have been accepted by Malachi's listeners. They would have responded: "Yes, we've heard that before!" The prophet simply attempts to speak of the certainty of Yahweh's coming, to claim that it would come unexpectedly (3:1), and to get the people to prepare for it by remaining loyal to the Lord and by showing proper attitudes and actions in worship and daily life. Only the person who has "returned" to the Lord will be able to endure the refining fire of judgment (3:2-5; 4:1) and will find the "sun of righteousness" rising "with healing in its wings" (4:2). The picture in this last phrase is of health, peace, and joy because of the presence of Yahweh (see 2 Samuel 23:4; Isaiah 60:1). The expectation for the return of Elijah (4:5-6) before the arrival of the messianic kingdom was identified with John the Baptist by the New Testament (Luke 1:17; compare Matthew 11:13-14; Mark 6:14-15).

What abiding message has Malachi left? The prophet betrays a narrow outlook, not atypical of the postexilic period, when looking to the day Yahweh will "tread down the wicked" as ashes under foot (4:3). Even the grand statement in 2:10: "Have we not all one father? Has not one God created us?" does not refer to some sense of familial unity among all nations, but it applies in Malachi's thought only to Israelites. Still Malachi reminds us that God has not worked apart from human beings with all their foibles. In the midst of all the troubles, the divine word was there, encouraging and giving hope to a despondent people, assuring them that there was still a future. Perhaps this is the most we can gain from the book. God uses men and women at certain times and places to meet particular needs, and what they saw and how they acted may not have particular relevance to later generations. It is enough to know that in spite of the prophet's humanness, a need in the divine ministry to persons was filled.

Yet there may be more to Malachi's message than assurance. The prophet says in 1:11: "For from the rising of the sun to its setting my name is great among the nations, and in every place incense is offered to my name, and a pure offering; for my name is great among the nations, says the LORD of hosts." This may be a claim that all true worship (that is, all worship of deity sincerely and honestly given, whatever the name used by the heathen) is really worship of Yahweh, the only God (see 1:14). If this is what the prophet means, then Malachi would be in line with Amos, who saw all nations responsible to God only in terms they were able to know (Amos 1–2) and who believed God's providence extended to the Philistines and Syrians (Amos 9:7; compare Acts 10:35; Romans 2:12-16). Also, Malachi's strong condemnation of divorce (2:10-16) shows a sensitivity of spirit in line with Jesus' own words (Mark 10:2-12). Although divorce was allowed (Deuteronomy 24:1-4), it was intended only for hardship cases. Malachi's contemporaries abused this; they were using the allowance as an excuse for their lust. In the process they were causing hardship and cruelty for the wives. This is the reason the compassionate God cries out: "I hate divorce" (2:16).

- How does one's response to God affect the fulfillment of God's promises? What is the biblical meaning of "hope" as seen in Isaiah 56–66? How does this affect your own present life and hope?
- What do the prophets mean by the "day of the LORD"? What implications could this have for our country?
- How does the Book of Jonah confront us today in regard to any situations in our community?
- When does interest in the institutional forms of worship and life become constructive and destructive? Think of specific examples in your church.

- What have you learned about interpreting the prophetic words regarding the future? Did they chart the future in terms of details or basic divine purposes?

Additional Resources

Dentan, Robert C. "The Book of Malachi." In *The Interpreter's Bible,* edited by George A. Buttrick et al., vol. 6, 1117-1144. Nashville: Abingdon Press, 1956.

Lacocque, Andre and Pierre. *The Jonah Complex.* Atlanta: John Knox Press, 1981.

McKenzie, John L. *Second Isaiah.* The Anchor Bible, vol. 20. Garden City, N.Y.: Doubleday, 1968.

Meyers, Carol L. and Eric M. *Haggai, Zechariah 1–8.* The Anchor Bible, vol. 25B. Garden City, N.Y.: Doubleday, 1987.

Petersen, David L. *Haggai and Zechariah 1–8, A Commentary.* Philadelphia: Westminister Press, 1984.

Westermann, Claus. *Isaiah 40–66.* Translated by David M. Stalker. Philadelphia: Westminster Press, 1969.

Whybray, R. N. *Isaiah 40–66.* New Century Bible Commentary. Grand Rapids: William B. Eerdmans, 1981.

Wolff, H. W. *Joel and Amos.* Edited by Dean McBridge. Translated by Waldemar Janzen. Philadelphia: Fortress Press, 1977.

Wolff, H. W. *Obadiah and Jonah.* Translated by Margaret Kohl. Minneapolis: Augsburg, 1986.

11

THE APOCALYPSE

Daniel

The Book of Daniel presents us with the only apocalyptic book in the Old Testament. Traces of apocalyptic genre appear elsewhere in the Old Testament (Isaiah 13–14; 24–27; Ezekiel 1–3; 28–39; Joel 2–3; Zechariah 9–14) and the New Testament (Revelation; Mark 13; First and Second Thessalonians), and there are many Jewish apocalypses (for example, Second Enoch, Fourth Ezra, and so forth). The Book of Daniel has maintained a strong grip on the interest and imagination of many readers, primarily because of its purported insight into the future. Elaborate chronological schemes leading to the end of the age have been devised from its pages. And who will not admit to a certain fascination and curiosity about that which lies ahead? Yet, in spite of this, the primary importance of the Book of Daniel has been obscured in the desperate concern to wrest dates and signs from the author's account. The book's profound message is, however, not easy to grasp. We need first to understand something about apocalyptic writing.

THE NATURE OF APOCALYPTIC WRITING

The word "apocalyptic" ("revelation," "disclosure") describes both a type of literature and a kind of eschatology. As a *type of literature,* apocalyptic is characterized by (1) an abundant use of symbolism to relate supernatural revelations regarding the course of history. Strange animal figures and great cosmic disturbances predominate. These revelations are given through visions, dreams, or journeys through heaven. This means that not all of the details are intended to be taken literally. Daniel saw a horrible beast with teeth of iron and claws of bronze, having eleven horns on its head (7:19-20). The book of Revelation describes heaven as having walls of jasper, gates of pearl, and streets of gold (21:15-21). These are clearly symbolic. (2) Apocalyptic is also esoteric; its message is intended to be kept secret until some later period (see Daniel 8:26; 12:9), and its author is concealed under a pseudonym (usually some ancient worthy like Moses or Ezra or Enoch).

As a *kind of eschatology,* apocalyptic (1) views the end of the world as cataclysmic, not gradual. The word "eschatology" means "a study of last things," and apocalyptic eschatology views the "last things" as involving a series of great natural and supernatural upheavals before the coming of God's kingdom. (2) The apocalyptists were also pessimistic about present history. The prophetic belief that God was working in history to bring events to a conclusion is replaced by a view that God has virtually abandoned contemporary history. Evil has taken over, and the righteous are suffering. Salvation lies in the future after God intervenes once again. So the message of the apocalyptist to the people was a "tract for hard times." Have hope; God will soon return.

THE BOOK OF DANIEL

The Book of Daniel does not share in all the characteristics of the apocalyptic literature of the ancient world. It shares in the type of literature, but not in all of its eschatological emphases. It sees the end of the world as cataclysmic (chapter 7), but, like the prophets, it has not lost the sense of God's hand in present history (3:26-28; 4:34-37; 6:16-28; 9:1-23). Another prophetic emphasis in Daniel is the concern over behavior. In most apocalyptic works outside the Bible there is an ethical passivity; they presume that God's people are already righteous. Daniel sounds a prophetic note when he confesses his own sin, as well as that of the people (9:1-20; 4:27).

1. The Historical Setting. The book claims to be an account of the life and predictions of a Hebrew exile named Daniel who was taken while still a lad into Babylonian captivity. It divides quite naturally into two parts—*stories* concerning the faithfulness of

Daniel and his companions under the testings of the Babylonians (chapters 1–6), and *visions* concerning the end of the age (chapters 7–12). Daniel peered into the future and saw the course of events from the exile to the end of the age. Very little is known about Daniel; indeed, we have no knowledge of the person apart from the book. Ezekiel mentions a Daniel, along with Noah and Job, who was noted for wisdom and righteousness (Ezekiel 14:14, 20; 28:3). However, this is not the sixth century Daniel of the book, for apart from a different spelling of the name (in Hebrew it is literally "Danel"), Ezekiel is referring to three worthy men who were ancient in his day. Ezekiel is probably alluding to the same Daniel mentioned in some fourteenth century B.C. documents discovered at the site of the ancient city of Ugarit in Syria.

Traditionally the book has been assumed to be a collection of Daniel's memoirs made during his court service from Nebuchadnezzar (605–562 B.C.) to Cyrus (550–530 B.C.). This is how the book appears on the surface and would indicate a date close to 530 B.C. The purpose of the book, then, would be to encourage faithfulness among the exiles by detailing the unfolding plan of God for the establishment of God's kingdom. But most scholars emphasize that the book is apocalyptic, and thus it uses figures of the past as spokespersons to another age. This would suggest a later date. Furthermore, there are other difficulties in maintaining the traditonal view. Quite a few historical inaccuracies occur in the descriptions of the period before the second century B.C. Daniel 1:1 states, for example, that "in the third year of the reign of Jehoiakim king of Judah, Nebuchadnezzar, king of Babylon, came to Jerusalem and besieged it." This disagrees, however, with 2 Kings 24:1-2 and Jeremiah 22 and 25 that a deportation took place at this time (605 B.C.). Such discrepancies suggest that the author of Daniel was living much later than the events described and at a time when many of the details had been forgotten. The fact that the author shows accurate and detailed information about the rule of the Greeks in the second century but is sketchy and inaccurate about the rule of the Persians and Greeks before this time, has led scholars to date the book between 168 and 165 B.C. This does not mean that all of the material is late. The stories in chapters 1–6, for example, may well have been circulating in Judah for many years when the author of Daniel brought them together and revised them in the second century B.C.

When Persian rule passed into Greek hands in 331 B.C., the Jews did not experience any particular change in their semi-independent status. Greek culture influenced them, but they remained relatively free. Even when Alexander the Great died in 323 B.C., and the Judean part of his empire came under his general Ptolemy, there was still no change. But when Antiochus III, a Greek ruler of the house of Seleucus, defeated the Ptolemies in 198 B.C., Judah's situation began to change. The Seleucids, particularly under Antiochus IV, Epiphanes (175–163 B.C.), started to force Greek life and religion on the Jews. Many of the aristocrats and priests welcomed the Greek culture, but the people as a whole resisted this threat to their faith. The problem was brought to a head in 167 B.C. when, in an attempt to counter resistance, Antiochus murdered many Jews in Jerusalem, forbade the observance of the sabbath, sacrifice, festival, and circumcision, and erected an altar to Zeus in the temple (see 1 Maccabees 1:29ff.; 2 Maccabees 5:24-26). This spark ignited open rebellion under the leadership of a priest named Mattathias (1 Maccabees 2:15ff.). For the next three years there was guerilla warfare which is usually called the "Maccabean" revolt, after the nickname of Judas, the son and successor of Mattathias. Finally in December 164 B.C. Jerusalem was captured by the Jews, and the temple was cleansed. This event has been celebrated ever since by the Jews as the feast of Hanukkah ("dedication"). Antiochus died shortly afterwards, but the struggle for Palestine continued until full independence was achieved in 142 B.C. The Jews remained free until Roman forces overran Jerusalem in 63 B.C.

2. The Message. The Book of Daniel was written during the brief period of intense persecution by Antiochus IV, Epiphanes. It was intended to encourage faithfulness to Yahweh and to give hope in the face of death by promising the imminent coming of God's kingdom. Antiochus had overreached himself and would soon be destroyed. So the author tried to show, through the example of Daniel and his friends, that loyalty to God is rewarded, while wickedness, seen in the persons of Nebuchadnezzar and Belshazzar, is punished. God would deal similarly with the situation in the days of Antiochus. The author gathered together some traditional stories that had been known among the Jews about an Israelite worthy named Daniel (1–6), reworked and expanded them, and combined them with the visions (7–12). These latter materials were written in the second century using the name of the ancient Daniel. This was done in order to link the faith and certainty of God's purposes expressed in the visions with the similar themes in the stories. Hence, the book is not a series of predictions of events from the days of the sixth century B.C., but instead it is a reinterpretation of history from the days of Antiochus in the second century B.C. Where the author does predict, it is in reference to the imminent coming of the kingdom of God after the death of Antiochus. The specific way in which the author saw the end of the present age did not take place. The kingdom did not come after the rule of the Greeks ended. Yet, as we have seen, neither were the prophets always correct about the form of the fulfillment of God's promises. Nevertheless, their theology and call for faith remain as abiding contributions, and they caution us not to attempt to run ahead of God and set times and ways that God must work.

Both the stories and the visions share in a common theme of God's sovereign control of all history. Those who remain faithful to God are guaranteed a place in the future. This theme is described in various ways.

- What are the differences between books of the prophets and the Book of Daniel of which we should be aware?
- Could the author of Daniel be incorrect about the specific time of the end of the age and still be correct about the certainty of that end?
- What particular aspects of Daniel's message speak to us today?

Additional Resources

Hartman, Louis F., and di Lella, Alexander A. *The Book of Daniel.* The Anchor Bible, vol. 23. Garden City, N.Y.: Doubleday, 1978.

Russell, D. S. *Daniel: An Active Volcano.* Louisville: Westminster/John Knox Press, 1990.

Welch, Adam C. *Visions of the End: A Study in Daniel and Revelation.* Naperville, Ill.: Alec R. Allenson, 1922.

Yamauchi, Edwin M. *Persia and the Bible.* Grand Rapids: Baker Book House, 1990.

NOTES

1. Roland deVaux, *Ancient Israel: Its Life and Institutions* (New York: McGraw-Hill Book Company, 1962), p. 493.

2. Norman Gottwald, *A Light to the Nations* (New York: Harper & Row, Publishers, Inc., 1959), p. 153.

3. John Bright, *A History of Israel* (Philadelphia: Westminster Press, 1959), pp. 209-271. See Edwin R. Thiele, *The Mysterious Numbers of the Hebrew Kings,* rev. ed. (Grand Rapids: William B. Eerdmans Publishing Company, 1965).

4. Gerhard von Rad, *Old Testament Theology,* vol. 1 (New York: Harper & Row, Publishers, Inc., 1962), p. 347.

5. *Ibid.,* p. 353.

6. George S. Gunn, *God in the Psalms* (Edinburgh: Saint Andrew Press, 1956), p. 207.

7. Claus Westermann, *Basic Forms of Prophetic Speech* (Philadelphia: Westminster Press, 1967), pp. 64-69.

8. W. O. E. Oesterley and Theodore H. Robinson, *An Introduction to the Books of the Old Testament* (New York: Macmillan Company, 1934), p. 367.

9. G. W. Anderson, *The History and Religion of Israel* (New York: Oxford University Press, 1966), p. 119.

10. Sheldon Blank, *Prophetic Faith in Second Isaiah* (New York: Harper & Row, Publishers, Inc., 1958), p. 186.

11. Gerhard von Rad, *Der Prophet Jona* (Nürnberg: Laetare—Verlag, 1950), p. 3.

12. Gerhard von Rad, *Old Testament Theology,* vol. 2. (London: Oliver and Boyd, 1965), pp. 281-282.

13. John Bright, *A History of Israel* (Philadelphia: Westminster Press, 1959), pp. 394-395.